Pelican Books
Lenin and the Russian Revolution

Christopher Hill was educated at St Peter's School, York, and at Balliol College, Oxford, where he received a 'first' in modern history in 1934. That year he was also made a fellow of All Souls College, Oxford. In 1936 he was assistant lecturer in modern history at University College, Cardiff, and two years later tutor in modern history at Balliol. During his war service he had a variety of posts: Field Security Police, Oxfordshire and Buckinghamshire Light Infantry, Intelligence Corps and the Foreign Office. He returned to Oxford in 1945 and from 1958 until 1965 was university lecturer in sixteenth- and seventeenth-century history. He was Ford Lecturer in English History in 1962. From 1965–78 he was Master of Balliol College. In 1978 he became Visiting Professor at the Open University. In 1965 he was made D. Litt., Oxon. Dr Hill, a Fellow of the Royal Historical Society and of the British Academy, was a member of the editorial board of *Past and Present* (1952–68), and since 1961 of the Yale University Press edition of the Complete Prose of John Milton. He was made Hon. D.Litt. of Hull in 1966; of Sheffield in 1967; of East Anglia in 1968; and of Glasgow and Bristol, 1976. His publications include *The English Revolution* (1940), *Economic Problems of the Church* (1956), *Puritanism and Revolution* (1958), *The Century of Revolution* (1961), *Society and Puritanism in Pre-Revolutionary England* (1964), *Intellectual Origins of the English Revolution* (1965), *Reformation to Industrial Revolution* (1967), which is Volume 2 in the series *The Pelican Economic History of Britain*, *God's Englishman: Oliver Cromwell and the English Revolution* (1970), *Antichrist in 17th Century England* (1971), *The World Turned Upside Down* (1972), *Change and Continuity in 17th Century England* (1974), and *Milton and the English Revolution* (1977) which won the Royal Society of Literature Award. He also contributed to *Rebels and their Causes*, a collection of essays to celebrate the seventy-fifth birthday of A.L. Morton. Dr Hill has travelled in Europe generally, in Japan and India and in the U.S.A. He is married, with three children.

Christopher Hill

Lenin and
the Russian Revolution

Penguin Books

Penguin Books Ltd, Harmondsworth,
Middlesex, England
Penguin Books, 625 Madison Avenue,
New York, New York 10022, U.S.A.
Penguin Books Australia Ltd, Ringwood,
Victoria, Australia
Penguin Books Canada Ltd, 2801 John Street,
Markham, Ontario, Canada L3R 1B4
Penguin Books (N.Z.) Ltd,
182–190 Wairau Road, Auckland 10, New Zealand

First published in the 'Teach Yourself History' series by
The English University Press 1947
Published in Pelican Books 1971
Reprinted 1978, 1980

Set, printed and bound in Great Britain by
Cox & Wyman Ltd, Reading
Set in Linotype Pilgrim

to Dona Torr

Contents

Introduction

I

At the beginning of 1917, Russia, in alliance with England, France and Japan, was at war with Germany. Her losses in two and a half years of war had been prodigious, and so far had produced no results. The troops were exhausted, badly equipped, badly led and for the most part quite unable to comprehend what the war was about. Twelve years earlier Russia's defeat in a war against Japan had produced a revolution against the autocracy of Tsar Nicholas II. This had been crushed, and certain concessions had been made, including the setting up of a representative assembly, the State Duma. But the franchise for this body was soon narrowed, and it enjoyed little real power: the Tsar's government continued to be corrupt and autocratic, and had forfeited the confidence of all classes of society.

On 12 March 1917, by an almost bloodless revolution in the capital, the government was overthrown. The provinces followed suit; the commanders-in-chief of the armies in the field united with the State Duma in calling on Nicholas to abdicate; and the three-hundred-year-old dynasty of the Romanovs quietly disappeared. A Provisional Government was set up, representing the conservative and liberal parties, who held a majority in the State Duma. The members of this government had not created the revolution; they merely occupied the vacant seats of authority. The real power in Petrograd soon came to be the Soviet, a revolutionary council of workers' deputies. Soviets also sprang up in the army and navy, in Moscow and provincial towns and in some country districts: ultimately a central Congress of Soviets was established in Petrograd, to which local soviets sent delegates. Meanwhile the Petrograd

Soviet was acting virtually as a second government, issuing orders of its own, which received more obedience in the army and amongst the working-class population than those of the Provisional Government. Freedom of the press and of assembly established themselves; revolutionary leaders were liberated from prison and returned from exile.

Among them came Lenin. He arrived in April, and at once began to attack the Provisional Government, to call for the ending of the war, for the distribution of land to the peasants and for the transfer of power to the soviets. The support which the Bolshevik party won for this programme brought the honeymoon phase of the revolution to an end. The Provisional Government was hastily reconstructed so as to draw in representatives of those parties in the Soviet which were prepared to continue the war. Kerensky became Prime Minister. An offensive was started. The Bolsheviks were proscribed, Lenin driven into hiding.

But the war aroused no enthusiasm. The Bolshevik slogan of 'Peace, bread and land' won more and more support. The armies at the front dissolved. In August an attempt at a counter-revolutionary coup by General Kornilov was defeated. But this episode revealed the weakness of Kerensky's government, which would have had no hope of resisting Kornilov's challenge without the support of the real power in Russia – the soviets of workers' and soldiers' deputies. Kerensky had hitherto held power by balancing right against left; now one side of the balance was empty. The Provisional Government had promised a redistribution of the land and a constituent assembly; it gave neither, and had nothing to offer in their place but patriotic and unpopular appeals to carry on the war. The Bolsheviks obtained a majority in the Petrograd Soviet. They already had an effective majority among the rank and file of the army. On 6 and 7 November the soviets took over power almost without opposition. A government was formed under Lenin, which at once issued laws giving the land to the peasants, nationalized key industries and announced its intention of ending the war by a peace without annexations and indemnities.

A treaty with the Germans was signed at Brest-Litovsk in March 1918, on very harsh terms. But there was no peace yet for war-weary Russia. The defeated survivors of the old régime were enabled by foreign military help to challenge the verdict of history, and for nearly three years there was fighting all over Russia. When finally the Soviet forces had defeated the 'fourteen nations', a long period of reconstruction was needed. The 'New Economic Policy' was introduced in 1921, and a slow recovery began. In the following year Lenin was paralysed by a stroke, and in January 1924 he died.

2

Such were the main events of the Russian Revolution down to Lenin's death. I hope that this summary may help the reader to follow the threads of the argument in the remainder of the book. Space did not permit me to write a history of the Russian Revolution, of which there are already many; nor have I tried to write a biography of Lenin. What I have attempted is an assessment of the place of Lenin, and of the revolution which was his life's work, in history: an ambitious enough task in all conscience. I have therefore selected for more detailed treatment those aspects of Lenin's activity and thought, and those achievements of the revolution, which seem to me to have more than local significance. The Bolshevik party itself, on account of the features which differentiate it from other socialist parties; the agrarian policy of this party in a country where peasants formed eighty per cent of the population; the political philosophy which inspired the revolution and the Soviet state; Lenin's critique of imperialism and his definition of the national and international policy which the rulers of the Soviet state should pursue – these seemed the subjects without some consideration of which it would be impossible to come to any understanding of the Russian Revolution.

For the sake of simplicity I have used the new style of dating throughout, although this was not adopted in Russia until after the Bolshevik Revolution. To convert dates to the old style twelve days should be subtracted in the nineteenth century and thirteen between 1900 and 14 (1) February 1918. But I have kept the traditional names February and October Revolution, although, in fact, these revolutions occurred in March and November respectively according to the Gregorian calendar (27 February old style, 12 March new style; 24 and 25 October old style, 6 and 7 November new style). Before 1914 I have referred to the capital of Russia as St Petersburg; it was then renamed Petrograd. Today of course we know it as Leningrad – Lenin's city.

In quoting Lenin's works I have normally used the standard English translations; but I have checked these translations with the original Russian (3rd edition) and in some cases made alterations, for which I alone am responsible.

Many people have helped me in writing this book. I should like to thank especially Miss Dorothy Marshall, Mr and Mrs Rodney Hilton, Mr Maurice Dobb, Mr Donald Pennington, Mr A. L. Rowse, the editor of the series to which this volume belongs, and above all Miss Dona Torr.

Part One
Before the Revolution

1 The Causes of the Revolution

'Much has been left in the world that *must* be destroyed by fire and iron.' (LENIN *in 1915*)

I

In 1917, in two revolutions, the Russian people dethroned their tsar, disestablished their state church, expropriated their aristocracy. In England and France these things were done rather earlier – in England in the Civil War of the seventeenth century, in France in the Revolution of 1789. So, in approaching the Russian Revolution, the question we must ask ourselves is not, Why did such violent events take place in Russia in 1917? – at a time when west European development was by comparison peaceful and constitutional – but why were these events so much longer delayed in Russia than in the West? The first question might lead us to suppose that there is something peculiarly Russian about bloody revolution, and before we know where we are we shall be talking nonsense about the Slav soul. There were some very Russian characteristics about the revolution of 1917; but it is important to get clear from the start that in it Russia was finishing with the Middle Ages in the same sort of way as we did in 1640 and as the French did in 1789. Then we can ask ourselves why Russia's development was so delayed.

The main reason is that she failed to produce an independent middle class. In western Europe the seventeenth, eighteenth and nineteenth centuries were the great age of capitalist expansion, during which the commercial and industrial classes took over first economic and then political power from the landed aristocracies and the absolute monarchies. Throughout the heroic age of Western capitalism, Russia was in an economic backwater;

her trade was in the hands of foreigners, her few industries run by the tsar or other landlords. Russia's middle class was very slow and late in developing, its dealings were on a small scale and its political independence was nil. So Liberalism, the philosophy of the rising bourgeoisie in the West, had no social roots in Russia. Power remained concentrated in the hands of the autocratic tsar, ruling through a rigid and corrupt bureaucracy and supported by an aristocracy which was omnipotent in the countryside and occupied all positions of importance in the army and civil service.

Liberalism's first chance in Russia came after the disastrous defeats of the Crimean War (1853–6). They showed that wars could no longer be won without a modern industry, and exposed the cumbrous disorganization of the state machine. A period of economic and political reforms began with the abolition of serfdom in 1861. But though some of the techniques of Western civilization were introduced from on top, the changes never had the backing of a competent and self-reliant middle class to put them into effect and give them reality at the lower levels of government. They proved to be largely a sham, a façade behind which the aristocracy and bureaucracy continued to monopolize power. There was no social stuff in Russia making for compromise.

Such liberal ideas as had penetrated the country came as part of an alien creed, accessible only to the well-to-do; and this creed was no longer unchallenged in the West. By 1861 the romantics were already attacking the ugliness of industrialism, the socialists the inequalities of Capitalism. So even of the earliest Russian opponents of tsarism few had any wish merely to take over the institutions and ideas of Western parliamentarism. The conservative Slavophils idealized the 'good old Slav customs', tried to make a virtue of the fact that Russia's social development had lagged three hundred years behind that of the West. A more democratic school of thinkers dreamed that Russia might pass directly into a kind of peasant anarchist-socialism, without undergoing industrialization – to which everything evil in Western capitalism was attributed. But these

'Narodniks', for all their mystic faith in 'the people' (*narod* in Russian), were themselves mostly 'penitent aristocrats', land-owners ashamed of living on the backs of the peasantry. In background, education and sympathies they were quite out of touch with and rather afraid of the real peasants. Those in-tellectuals of the seventies and eighties who 'went to the people', to live and work in the villages, found it extremely difficult even to make themselves understood by the illiterate and priest-ridden peasants, whose political philosophy was lim-ited to a dim religious hope that the tsar, a being as distant and hypothetical as God, would one day relieve their misery and punish their oppressors. But as the Russian proverb has it, 'God is high in heaven, the tsar is far away': the landlord continued to be very much on the spot.

Social changes came with the rapid industrial development of the last three decades of the nineteenth century. But this was almost entirely financed by foreign capital, and had little effect on the position of the native middle class. Dependent on the West alike for capital, technicians and political ideas, the Rus-sian bourgeoisie had to invoke the protection of the tsarist state against their economically more powerful rivals. They had no thought of challenging the political dominance of the mon-archy and gentry until, in the twentieth century, the régime again revealed, under the stress of modern war, its utter incom-petence and corruption, its inability even to maintain order and financial stability.

2

By this time another power had appeared on the scene – the working-class movement which industrialization created. The Russian proletariat, dragged from its pauper plots of land, hurled into the factories and mines, herded into insanitary bar-racks, grossly underpaid and overworked, rapidly came to con-sciousness of itself in conditions most favourable to combination, class solidarity, organization and the development of a mass revolutionary movement. Because capitalist development came so late in Russia, many branches of industry stepped at once from the handicraft stage to the big factory with the most modern equipment. The factories tended to be run either by foreign firms, interested principally in quick returns, or by less efficient native capitalists, who could compete only by cutting costs: there were more casualties each year in Russian factories than during the whole of the Russo-Turkish War of 1877–8. So the class struggle was especially naked.

Unlike the middle class, the Russian proletariat inherited from the West an ideology which had not outlived its vitality. The revolutions of 1848 and the Paris Commune of 1871, together with the theoretical writings of Marx and Engels and the political experience of the parties of the Second International, had produced a body of socialist doctrine and traditions of a specifically working-class revolution. Such a 'proletarian revolution', according to the Marxist theory which Lenin adopted, would establish socialism through the rule of the working class, just as the 'bourgeois revolutions' of 1640 and 1789 had led to the rule of the middle class.*

So far I have been trying to answer the question with which I started: Why did the revolution abolishing absolutism and the survivals of feudalism come so much later in Russia than in England and France? This leads us to ask a further question: Why did a socialist revolution, superseding capitalism and liberal parliamentary government, succeed in a country like Russia, relatively backward industrially, at a time when working-class parties in Western Europe were acting either as legal parliamentary oppositions or as offshoots of still more respectable liberal parties? At this stage I shall do no more than indicate the question. It was one with which Lenin occupied himself a great deal, and his answer should become apparent in what follows. But one point is already clear. In England, France and Germany, thanks to the maturity and strength of the liberal tradition, the working-class movement tended to become swallowed up in

---

*I shall continue to use the Marxist term 'bourgeois revolution' and 'proletarian revolution' as convenient shorthand expressions.

parliamentary and 'reformist' activities. In Russia, where there was no such tradition, and where there was no hope of winning reforms by constitutional means, even the aristocratic and intellectual radicals became revolutionaries and terrorists in the seventies and eighties. From its first beginnings the leaders of the working-class movement in Russia assumed, and rightly assumed, that a violent overthrow of the existing régime was a necessary preliminary to obtaining the reforms which they demanded. The words of the Communist Manifesto were almost literally true of the Russian factory workers: they had nothing to lose but their chains; they had a world to win.

3

The revolution was made against the autocracy of the tsars, a type of government which we in England have not known since the seventeenth century. There had been special reasons for the survival of such a régime in Russia. The country was always too large, and its communications too bad, for it to be efficiently administered from a single centre. Yet military defence in that country of flat open plains demanded a highly centralized government under a single leader; and the autocracy subsequently survived to give some uniformity of administration for the medley of backward and illiterate peoples who composed the vast Russian Empire.

By the end of the nineteenth century the steam engine and the telegraph had made autocracy a complete anachronism. But institutions tend to survive long after the reason for their existence has vanished. Nicholas II still adhered in the twentieth century to the notion that he was tsar by divine right and that it was his moral duty not to allow the structure of absolutism to be tampered with, since it would stand or fall as a whole. In a sense he was right.

The Russian state was the negation of democracy; but democracy could not be introduced without at the same time permitting a development of capitalism. For the possibility of introducing responsible self-government into Russia depended in the first instance on improving communications. Until education, and political education, could be pushed into outlying villages with the help of railways and the telephone, local self-government could not but be unreal; until aeroplanes and later wireless had made quick reference to the capital possible, the hands of the bureaucracy could not be untied to deal with individual cases.

For the bureaucracy could not bend, could not adapt itself. Its inextricable entanglement with the class rule of the gentry and its determined attitude of 'after us the deluge' meant that it found itself in opposition to the development of those forces of production which alone could have created the conditions in which bureaucratic government could have been modified. Hence the revolution. The development of a respect for human personality in Russia, paradoxically, depends in the first instance on the diffusion of technological inventions. Or, as Lenin put it in one of those epigrams of his which flash a light over large tracts of obscurity: 'Electrification is the basis of democracy.'

The fundamental cause of the Russian Revolution, then, was the incompatibility of the tsarist state with the demands of modern civilization. War accelerated the development of revolutionary crises, but their deep-lying causes could not be wished away in times of peace. So in 1904 we find the Minister of the Interior (whose department was responsible for the maintenance of order) advocating 'a small victorious war' as the only means of averting revolution. Instead, an unsuccessful war against Japan produced the revolution of 1905; the defeats of 1914–17 led straight to the final catastrophe of 1917. 'The revolution took place,' wrote Mr Bruce Lockhart, who saw it, 'because the patience of the Russian people broke down under a system of unparalleled inefficiency and corruption.'

But if war was the immediate cause of the revolution of 1917, the circumstances in which the tsarist government entered the war of 1914–18 were the outcome of Russia's historical backwardness. The capital needed to finance her rapid industrial and railway development and to employ the millions of labourers set free by the 'Emancipation' of 1861 had come from abroad. Before 1914 all the big power stations in Russia were in foreign hands, as well as ninety per cent of the joint stock of her mining industries. English and French capital built the Russian railways; French capital predominated in the coal and metallurgy of the Ukraine, British in the oil of the Caucasus. Germany, occupied with her own rapid expansion after the Franco-Prussian War, had less capital available for export, and was not anxious to have a heavily industrialized Russia as her eastern neighbour; so French bankers became the principal creditors of Russia. As Europe divided into two rival camps these loans acquired a political significance.

The decisive year was 1906, the first year of the constitution extorted from Nicholas II by the revolution of 1905. In his Manifesto of 30 October 1905, the tsar had promised 'to establish as an unchangeable principle that no law can obtain force without the consent of the State Duma and that to the elected of the people there should be granted the possibility of actual participation in supervision of the legality of the actions of the authorities appointed by Us'. If this promise had been carried out, the Duma might have hoped to win control of state expenditure, and so of government policy. But Nicholas had other ideas. In April 1906 a syndicate of bankers, mainly French and with the backing of the French government, granted the tsar's government a loan of 2,250 million francs – 'the largest loan yet made in the history of mankind,' the Russian Prime Minister proudly called it.

Henceforth Nicholas could snap his fingers at the State Duma. When the representative assembly of the people of Russia met a month later, the first Bill which the government asked it to consider was a grant for the construction of a library and greenhouse at a provincial university. The State Duma was dissolved after sitting for two months. At the end of 1905 the St Petersburg Soviet had threatened that the victorious revolution would repudiate the debts of the tsar's government. The opposition members of the Duma now retired to the comparative freedom of Finland and called on the country to refuse to pay taxes or to recognize foreign loans concluded without the Duma's consent. But there was no response. The revolution had been defeated, and the dividends of French investors seemed to have been secured.

The price was soon paid. Whilst the negotiations for the loan were proceeding, the Algeciras Conference had been in session. Here England and France were opposing German ambitions in Morocco, and the Russian representatives, at the specific instance of Nicholas II, had been directed to vote for France: Germany had to withdraw in face of an Anglo-French-Russian bloc. In the next year England's long-standing disagreements with Russia were patched up, and the two sides had lined up as they were to fight in 1914.

4

War inevitably strengthened the position of the bourgeoisie, which had prospered with the belated but rapid development of capitalism in Russia. It also strengthened the position of the State Duma. Only the latter, in collaboration with the Union of Zemstvos and the Union of Cities, could mobilize the drive and energy necessary to produce munitions, military equipment and Red Cross supplies on the scale required. The Prime Minister told the President of the Duma (Rodzyanko) that food and munitions were no concern of his and that he 'could not interfere in matters concerning the war'. When Rodzyanko wished to organize a meeting of mayors and heads of zemstvos at the request of the commander-in-chief, in order to accelerate the supply of boots for the army, it was forbidden by the Minister of the Interior, who thought the real object of the meeting was to agitate for a constitution. General Brusilov, who complained bitterly of the shortage of all kinds of military equipment, noted that the Minister of War engaged in permanent hostilities with the Duma instead of collaborating.

Under these circumstances it was difficult for patriots who disliked the idea of soldiers going barefoot not to entertain subversive thoughts. Just because the war strengthened the business classes, there were many in governmental and court circles (including the tsaritsa) who were most unenthusiastic about it, and wished for a separate peace with Wilhelm II, with whose system of government they had much more sympathy than with English and French parliamentarism.

As the war proceeded the incompetence (to say the least) of the governments appointed by the tsar, and the necessity of keeping Russia in the war, forced the English and French Ambassadors more and more to ally with the State Duma and the liberal opposition. They pressed the tsar to release the frustrated energies of the country and swing them in being with the war effort by cooperating with Russian representative institutions. Lenin (and many others) suspected that the English and French Ambassadors engineered the revolution of February 1917. This may not have been literally true, for Sir George Buchanan at all events was shrewd enough to see that a revolution once started would be difficult to stop; but it was a correct statement of the logic of the situation. Certainly the government which was formed as a result of the February Revolution was linked by the closest ties with England and France. It was utterly dependent on them for the military supplies which alone could keep Russia in the war and win for her the control of the Straits and the other territorial gains promised by the secret treaties. But by this time it was already too late for the Western capitalist powers to save the monarchy.

There was indeed much to be said for the view expressed by Lenin that only the extrication of Russia from the war and the repudiation of foreign debts – i.e. a much more thorough-going revolution than that of February 1917, which brought to power a liberal government based on the Duma – could establish Russia's national independence. In 1916 the interest and sinking fund on the state debt amounted to more than the whole state revenue: half of this was directly due to foreign banks and governments, and the foreign debt was increasing rapidly.

5

At the age of twenty-five Lenin had sketched a draft programme for the still non-existent Russian Social-Democratic party. In an 'Explanation' appended to this draft he included a remarkable passage on the effects of foreign investment (then just beginning) on the development of the Russian Revolution.

Lately, foreign capitalists have been eagerly investing their capital in Russia; they are establishing branch factories here and are forming companies for the purpose of establishing new enterprises in Russia. They are flinging themselves hungrily upon a young country in which the government is even more friendly and obliging to capital than elsewhere, where the workers are less united and less able to resist them than in Western countries, and where the standard of living (and consequently wages) is lower, so that the foreign capitalists can obtain higher profits here than they ever dreamed of obtaining in their own countries. International capital is reaching out to Russia. The Russian workers are stretching out their hands to the international labour movement.

To summarize the argument: the development of capitalism in late nineteenth-century Russia created the conditions for a revolution against the tsarist state. Simultaneously the backwardness of native capitalism and the weakness of the landowners' government made Russia attractive to foreign investors. Foreign investment accelerated the growth of capitalism in Russia, and with it the development of a working-class movement which linked up with and learnt from the workers' movement of the West. It was fear of the working-class movement in Russia which in 1906 made the French government come to the help of tsarism. The tsar was propped up against a bourgeois revolution lest the latter should go too far. But when the tsar's government paid the price by participating in the war against Germany, the interests both of the capitalists inside Russia and of the Western capitalist states coincided in fostering a development of liberal parliamentarism and bourgeois control, which finally produced the revolution of February 1917.

But the interests of native capitalists and foreign investors converged too late. By that time the working-class movement had developed to a point at which it was able to sweep aside the weak liberal government, which had as little social basis inside Russia as the tsarist government in its last days: and with the advent of the Bolsheviks in November 1917 Russian capitalism and foreign investments disappeared together. 'History', the poet Blok had warned the Russian intelligentsia nine years earlier, 'that same history which, they say, can be reduced simply to political economy, has placed a real bomb on the table.'

6

So far we have been dealing with the larger, more impersonal causes of the Russian Revolution. But long-term causes work their effects through human agencies: the immediate reasons for the Russian Revolution centre round the personality of the tsar, Nicholas II. Nicholas was, by all accounts, a good husband and a good father. So were Charles I of England and Louis XVI of France, who in similar historical circumstances also found that private virtues were no substitute for political sense – or, one may add, for political honesty: Nicholas shared Charles I's view that an appeal to his coronation oath absolved him from the most solemn engagement if it suited him. And that meant, of course, if it suited the tsaritsa: for Nicholas, who lacked all traces of will or character, was entirely under the influence of his wife. This further irony of history has often been noted: Charles I, Louis XVI and Nicholas II were all devoted to and dominated by hated foreign wives, whose political interferences and ineptitude converted their ruin from probability to certainty: the Frenchwoman, l'Autrichienne, Nemka (the German woman). But there the historical parallel ceases: neither Laud nor Cagliostro can decently be compared with Rasputin, the unspeakable blackguard who ruled the tsaritsa as she ruled her husband.

Rasputin was notoriously debauched, certainly corrupt, and probably at least used by German agents. Yet through the

tsaritsa he was able to get his friends made bishops and arch-
bishops and even to create an entirely new saint; in the end he
practically dictated the formation of governments, and thus
directly influenced the conduct of policy and the war. Full
reports on Rasputin's debaucheries were made available to the
tsar, but he refused to accept them, and the well-meaning tale-
bearers fell from favour. The press was (quite illegally) forbidden to mention Rasputin's name. Some may regard it as a
mitigating circumstance that the tsaritsa's relations with Rasputin were undoubtedly wholly innocent: he had some curious
hypnotic influence over her haemophilic son, and this convinced the hysterical mother that Rasputin was 'a man of
God'.

The tsaritsa's letters to her husband, written when he was
away with the army and she was virtually head of the home
government, must be read before the extent of Rasputin's sway
can be grasped. The merits of cabinet ministers, chiefs of staff,
the commander-in-chief himself were tested entirely by their
attitude to Rasputin.

'Can't you realize that a man [the Grand Duke Nicholas] who
turned simple traitor to a man of Gods, cannot be blessed, nor
his actions be good?' the tsaritsa wrote on June 1915;* two
months later the Grand Duke was dismissed from the post of
commander-in-chief, which the tsar took over himself, against
the written advice of eight of his ministers. Brusilov considered
that this action sealed the fate of the monarchy: henceforth the
army's defeats were the direct responsibility of the tsar. In February 1916 the tsaritsa secured the appointment of a totally
incompetent Prime Minister, Stürmer, who, as one of his friends
put it, thought that 'the war with Germany was the greatest
possible misfortune for Russia and had no serious political
justification'. The tsaritsa, on the other hand, wrote that
Stürmer 'very much values Gregory [Rasputin] which is a great
thing'. In November 'Our Friend [Rasputin] says Stürmer can

---

*The grammar and punctuation are the tsaritsa's. She wrote in
English, but thought in German.

remain still some time as Prime Minister,' but that he should cease to be Minister of Foreign Affairs. He ceased.

The appointment most outrageous to public opinion was that of Protopopov, a renegade liberal member of the State Duma who was also reputedly pro-German, to be Minister of the Interior in September 1916. The tsaritsa recommended him for this key post in the following remarkable words. 'He likes our Friend since at least four years, & that says much for a man. ... I don't know him but I believe in our Friend's wisdom and guidance. ... Do listen to Him who only wants your good & whom God has given more insight, wisdom and enlightenment than all the military put together.' The tsar was still uneasy: but after Rasputin had 'shouted a bit', Protopopov was appointed. Through him Rasputin directly controlled internal policy. The tsaritsa wrote a month after this appointment: 'Forgive me for what I have done – but I had to – our Friend said it was *absolutely* necessary. Protopopov is in despair because he gave you that paper the other day, thought he was acting rightly until Gr[egory] told him it was quite wrong. So I spoke to Stürmer yesterday & they both completely believe in our Friend's wonderful, God sent wisdom. Stürmer sends you by this messenger a new paper to sign' – which put Protopopov, to his own embarrassment, in charge of food supplies for the whole of Russia. The revolution came four months later.

Not only were the ministers shockingly incompetent, they were also changed with bewildering rapidity as the situation went from bad to worse. In the two years before the February Revolution there were four Prime Ministers, six Ministers of the Interior, four Ministers of War and four of Agriculture. This 'ministerial leapfrog' in time of war and acute internal crisis contributed no less than the arbitrary interferences of the tsaritsa and Rasputin to prevent the orderly working of the government departments.

Not that we should attribute too much to the personal corruption of Rasputin himself: he was the symbol of a far deeper corruption in Russian society. Rodzyanko, who in his capacity of President of the State Duma continually and vainly tried to open the tsar's eyes to the abyss that was ever widening between the court and decent opinion in Russia, wrote in measured terms:

> The appearance at Court of Gregory Rasputin, and the influence he exercised there, mark the beginning of the decay of Russian society and the loss of prestige for the throne and for the person of the tsar himself. . . . The blame for the process of disruption which began to manifest itself at this time cannot be laid upon the Emperor Nicholas II alone. The burden of responsibility rests fully on those members of the ruling classes who, blinded by their ambition, cupidity and desire for advancement, forgot the terrible danger which was threatening their Emperor and Russia.

7

Lenin subsequently defined 'the fundamental law of revolution' in the following words: 'It is not sufficient for revolution that the exploited and oppressed masses understand the impossibility of living in the old way and demand changes; for revolution, it is necessary that the exploiters should not be able to live in the old way. . . . It follows that for revolution it is essential, first, that a majority of the workers (or at least a majority of the class-conscious, thinking, politically active workers) should fully understand that revolution is necessary and be ready to sacrifice their lives for it; secondly, that the ruling classes be in a state of governmental crisis which draws even the most backward masses into politics (a symptom of every real revolution is the rapid, tenfold and even hundredfold increase in the number of representatives of the toiling and oppressed masses – who hitherto have been apathetic – capable of waging the political struggle), a crisis which weakens the government and makes it possible for the revolutionaries to overthrow it rapidly.'

This law, Lenin added, was confirmed by the revolution of 1905 and the two revolutions of 1917. Since the beginning of the century the autocracy's normal technique of administration had included the employment on a wide scale of agents-provocateurs, who organized strikes and political assassinations; and of the Black Hundreds, proto-fascist gangs who organized pogroms against Jews and socialists. A government which employed such methods in time of peace was clearly at war with a large section of its own people, and had forfeited the loyalty of decent elements even among the propertied classes. M. Maisky relates some revealing incidents from his schooldays in Omsk in the 1890s. One day his form discussed with their master, as schoolboys very properly do from time to time, whether the study of the classics was either useful or desirable. Within a short time the discussion turned into a heated *political* argument, in which all authority as such was questioned, and a row ensued which echoed all over the town. Soon afterwards an essay on literature in the reign of Catherine II produced political criticisms of censorship in general which authority chose to regard as a riot: the 'ringleader' was expelled.

This was symbolic of pre-revolutionary Russia. There was a complete divergence between the official machine of state, church and political police on the one hand, and the intelligentsia (indeed the mass of the population) on the other. Free thought was rebellion, and any normal-thinking person was bound sooner or later to run up against repression, as M. Maisky did at school, and as Lenin did at the university. (The universities, in fact, regularly turned out a quota of revolutionaries. The Narodnik terrorists of the seventies and eighties were drawn largely from this source, and many of the Bolshevik leaders first entered politics through the student movement.)

The government of Nicholas II was terrified of any thought or action which it did not control. In 1912, a famine year, the government stubbornly opposed the distribution of relief by other than official bodies. The censorship confiscated the programme of the harmless liberal Cadet party. Tolstoy was excommunicated by a church whose priests were required to disclose the secrets of the confessional when the interests of the State required it. In December 1906 the Most Holy Synod called upon priests to explain to their flocks the desirability of electing sound monarchists to the State Duma. The clergy were found in

1917 to be the class in the countryside which had the greatest sympathy for the old régime. A standing instruction to the police ordered them to keep observation over arguments against the dogmas of the Orthodox Church and over the conversion of the orthodox to other faiths.

As in England in 1640 and in France in 1789 a class of dissenters added to the inflammable material. Some of them, for conscientious reasons, refused to pay taxes, to perform military service or to pray for the tsar. Others preached the equality of man and advocated the equal division of all wordly goods. Some dissenting communities had communal flocks and herds and common granaries, from which each took according to his needs. The state church bitterly persecuted such dangerous persons, even to the extent of removing children from their parents. Forcible 'conversion' was not infrequent. The dissenters thus could not but support a revolution which brought them freedom of worship. Nor should we forget the thirty million Moslems in Russia, whose national and cultural institutions, religious beliefs and customs, were formally guaranteed for the first time in December 1917.

The Russia of the generation before the revolution, the Russia in which Lenin reached maturity, was the Russia of Chekhov: a class-ridden society in which decent human relations were thwarted by considerations of rank, by political and religious oppression, by jealousy and by bumbledom. A question which Chekhov's characters are continually asking was formulated helplessly by the undertaker in the story Rothschild's Fiddle: 'Why was the order of the world so strange that life, which is given to men only once, passes away without benefit?' But the helplessness was, at least in part, assumed in order to dupe the censorship: the hero of An Anonymous Story said cautiously but clearly: 'I believe it will be easier for the generations to come; our experience will be at their service. . . . One wants to make history so that those generations may not have the right to say of us that we were nonentities or worse.' To talk of the future in Russia was to criticize the present ('the order of the world'). No one has better captured the malaise, the frustration,

the fumbling hopes of a pre-revolutionary society than
Chekhov.

8

In July 1914 a strike movement in St Petersburg had culminated
in barricade fighting between police and workers. For a short
time the outbreak of war brought a revival of loyalty to the
throne; but the studied hostility of the tsar and his ministers to
all forms of representative government, together with the military defeats of the army which the tsar commanded and the
steady deterioration in the economic situation, which soon got
quite beyond the government's control, produced a violent
swing in the opposite direction. And the régime had no reserves
of goodwill to draw upon.

Between 1913 and 1917 nominal wages in industry trebled;
but they still lagged so far behind prices that they would purchase less than forty-five per cent of the goods which the same
wages would have bought in 1913. At the front, millions of
soldiers were killed and maimed, without having the slightest
idea what the war was about. They regarded it as a whim of the
tsar's; and when they saw that all their heroic efforts (e.g. Brusilov's offensive of 1916) produced no results because of the incompetence of the higher command, they began to ask why
they should go on sacrificing their lives to no purpose. This was
beginning to be true even of the officers, who by this time, after
heavy casualties in all ranks, were largely intellectuals in uniform. By 1916 over a million and a half deserters had been
posted.

Well might the Cadet (liberal) Milyukov demand in the State
Duma in November 1916 whether the ministers were guilty of
madness or treason. In December, in a last desperate effort to
save the autocracy from itself, Rasputin was murdered by a
Grand Duke, a prince who had married into the royal family,
and a reactionary member of the State Duma; at least one
leader of the Cadets was cognizant of the crime. But then it was
too late. Three months later the autocracy was swept away by

an almost completely spontaneous mass movement of workers and soldiers in Petrograd, which no one has ever claimed the credit for organizing. A Provisional Government was set up, representing the liberal opposition parties who had a majority in the State Duma. This government bowed to the prevalent radicalism by publishing a manifesto which promised freedom of speech, press, assembly and organization; the right to strike; the abolition of all class and national privileges; the organization of a people's militia with elected officers; elections for local government bodies and a Constituent Assembly on the basis of universal, equal, direct and secret suffrage. The tsar abdicated.

> Like the chewed stump of a fag
> We spat their dynasty out,

wrote Mayakovsky.

But side by side with the Provisional Government, representing the respectable classes, who hoped to profit by the revolution they had not dared to make, was the Petrograd Soviet, representing the organized workers and soldiers. The President of the State Duma wept when he heard that Russia was without a government: he rightly supposed that horrible responsibilities would be thrust upon him. But in Switzerland there was joy and a new hope among the Russian émigrés. Negotiations were opened for the return of Lenin to Russia across Germany in a 'sealed train'. He knew that the opportunity for which he had worked and waited for thirty years had arrived.

Who was Lenin?

2 Lenin (1870–1917)

'One cannot be a revolutionary Social-Democrat without participating according to one's powers in developing this theory (Marxism) and adapting it to changed conditions.'
(LENIN *in* 1915)

I

Vladimir Ilyich Ulyanov (Lenin) was born in 1870 at Simbirsk on the middle Volga, in the heart of Russia. Less than a century earlier the last of the great popular revolts, led by Pugachov, had drawn much of its support from this area, not only from the Russian peasantry, but also from the many non-Russian peoples whose descendants were still living on the banks of the Volga when Vladimir Ilyich grew up. Lenin's father, who died in 1886, was a physics teacher, who became an Inspector of Elementary Schools for Simbirsk Province the year before Vladimir was born, later rising to be Director of Elementary Schools for the same province. Vladimir's mother, who lived until a year before the Bolshevik Revolution, had been a schoolmistress: both parents were persons of enlightened views. They had six children, the five survivors of whom, as they grew up in the fierce repression of the eighties, seem almost automatically to have become revolutionaries. Vladimir's elder brother, Alexander, was a terrorist, who in 1887 was implicated in a plot to assassinate Alexander III: he was executed at the age of nineteen. This tragedy made a deep impression on Vladimir, who had loved and admired Alexander. The two brothers had already had many discussions on politics, and Lenin (as it will be convenient to call him, although he did not adopt the pseudonym until 1902) had already decided against terrorist methods. 'No, that is not the way we must go,' he is reported to have said when he heard of his brother's death. It is typical of him that from a personal tragedy he drew political conclusions: the subjective note is altogether missing from his writings and his thought.

Lenin had a normal middle-class education. His headmaster at Simbirsk high school, ironically enough, was the father of the Alexander Kerensky whose government the Bolsheviks were to overthrow in 1917. The elder Kerensky described Lenin as 'the pride of the school', and singled out for special praise his 'unusual carefulness and industry', his 'systematic thought' and the 'conciseness, clarity and simplicity of his exposition'. Nevertheless, as the brother of a terrorist, Lenin was only just accepted by the faculty of law at the local university, Kazan. That was in August 1887. Four months later, after a student riot, he and others were sent down.

Lenin's behaviour on this occasion, even in the official report of a member of the educational board of the Kazan district, does not sound wholly depraved.

He attracted attention by his secretiveness, inattentiveness and indeed rudeness. Two days before the riotous assembly he gave grounds for suspecting that he was meditating some improper behaviour: he spent much time in the common room, talking to the less desirable students, he went home and came back again with some object which the others had asked for, and in general behaved very strangely. And on 4 December he burst into the assembly hall among the leaders, and he and Polyansky were the first to rush shouting into the corridor of the second floor, waving their arms as though to encourage the others. ... In view of the exceptional circumstances of the Ulyanov family, such behaviour by Ulyanov ... gave reason to believe him fully capable of unlawful and criminal demonstrations of all kinds.

Naturally, after such shocking conduct, Vladimir Ilyich was exiled to a small estate of his mother's in the depth of the country.

Henceforth Lenin was under continuous police supervision. He was refused permission to enter any other university, and it was only three years later that he was allowed to take his legal examination as an external student of St Petersburg University. In 1891 he was awarded a first-class diploma in law, passing out first of thirty-three external students. Lenin alone obtained the highest mark on every subject. He had previously received permission first to return from the country to Kazan, then to move to Samara, also on the middle Volga. Here, in January 1892, he set up in practice as assistant to a liberal barrister. Records exist of twelve cases which Lenin defended in that year, although he secured acquittals only for two boys of thirteen. Most of the defendants seem to have been peasants goaded to acts of petty crime by poverty resulting from the famine of 1891. But Lenin must have got a certain political satisfaction from the defence of his first client – a tailor who was sentenced to one year's imprisonment for blasphemy. In the words of the indictment, 'he cursed the blessed Virgin, the Mother of God, the Holy Trinity, and also our sovereign Lord the Emperor and his heir-apparent, saying that our Lord the Emperor managed his affairs badly.'

These, however, are the mere externals of Lenin's life. At his mental development we can only guess. We know that his brother's death affected him deeply. Lenin later told his wife (whom he first met in 1893) what a fierce contempt he had come to feel for those 'liberal' friends of the Ulyanov family who had dropped them entirely after Alexander Ilyich's arrest and would not lift a finger to help the widow to secure a reprieve. In December 1887 Vladimir Ilyich confided to his fellow-students that he intended to become a professional revolutionary. Next year he was reading his dead brother's copy of Marx's *Capital*, and joined an illegal Marxist discussion circle in Kazan. In preparing for his examination Lenin had to study political economy and statistics, as well as purely legal subjects. He was asked questions about slavery in ancient Russia, about Russian representative institutions, including the village commune, about different forms of wages, about the Russian budget, about the rights of neutrals in international law – as well as about 'the philosophy of the police'. All this suggests that Lenin's university training may have proved of more use in his subsequent career than is often the case. Moreover, his visit to St Petersburg in 1891 to sit for the examination gave Lenin the opportunity to make contact with a group of Marxists there, unobserved by the highly incompetent police spies.

In the autumn of 1893 the Ulyanov family moved to Moscow, and Lenin himself went to St Petersburg. For the sake of appearances he was attached to the bar there, but he seems to have devoted most of his time to political work. He joined a group of Marxist intellectuals which was beginning to get in touch with factory workers through study circles. Lenin already enjoyed some reputation as a theoretician, and in 1894 issued (illegally) his first large-scale work, *What the Friends of the People are*. This was a criticism of the Narodniks and a plea for the foundation of a Russian Social-Democratic party.

But Lenin was soon dissatisfied with theoretical propaganda and began to press the 'old men' of the St Petersburg group to make contact with wider masses of workers. He wrote leaflets for factory workers on strike, which the group distributed. In May 1895 Lenin went abroad to ask Plekhanov and other émigrés to supply illegal literature for the Russian movement from abroad, and to discuss the possibility of founding a party. As a first step a 'League of Struggle for the Emancipation of the Working Class' was established in St Petersburg on Lenin's return; similar leagues grew up in other industrial centres. Preparations were made for issuing an illegal newspaper. The first number, mostly written by Lenin, was actually ready for the press when he and many other leading figures in the St Petersburg League were arrested (December 1895).

Lenin was kept in prison for over a year, during which period he continued to produce pamphlets and proclamations, writing them in milk, using 'inkwells' made of bread, which could be swallowed when necessary. But he was very lonely. We first meet his future wife, Nadezhda Konstantinovna Krupskaya, standing for hours on one particular spot of the pavement outside the prison in the hope that Lenin might catch a glimpse of her through a window whilst the prisoners took exercise.

When he was at length brought to trial Lenin was sentenced to three years' exile in Siberia, at Shushenskoye, near Minusinsk, in the Yenisei Province. Apart from the severe climate, and the fact that escape was impossible in that desolate and inaccessible region, the terms of his exile were not unduly harsh. He was able to obtain books for study, wrote a great deal and completed his *Development of Capitalism in Russia*. Once a week he gave free legal advice to peasants. In May 1898 he was joined by Krupskaya, who had also been sentenced to exile, and whom he married in Siberia.

Krupskaya was a school teacher, already active in the revolutionary movement before Lenin came to St Petersburg. From her arrival at Shushenskoye she shared Lenin's life, in eighteen long years of exile, and for seven years when her husband was head of the Soviet state and Krupskaya an official in the People's Commissariat for Education. She was Lenin's collaborator and secretary as well as his wife: and her *Memories of Lenin* – our primary source after his own writings – are deliberately impersonal and unemotional. Yet, for all her reticence, it is clear that her strength, calmness and understanding were a necessary background to Lenin's political life. After each party squabble during the bitter years of emigration Lenin and Krupskaya shouldered their rucksacks and went off to walk in the mountains somewhere until Lenin's nerves were restored.

When Lenin was finally released from Siberia, in February 1900, he at once took up the struggle where he had left it in 1895. After five months resuming old contacts he left for Switzerland to make arrangements for the publication abroad and smuggling into Russia of the illegal newspaper which it had proved impossible to print in Russia itself. In December 1900 the first number of *Iskra* (The Spark) appeared, and Lenin remained abroad on its editorial board. In July and August 1903 a party congress was held abroad, at which took place the famous split between Bolsheviks and Mensheviks; henceforth Lenin was in effect the leader of an independent Bolshevik party. During the revolution of 1905 he returned to St Petersburg, where he lived a semi-legal existence, taking little public part in revolutionary activities, but extremely active as a publicist and behind the scenes. With the defeat of the revolution Lenin withdrew to Finland, and finally left Russia with the police on his track in December 1907. For the next nine years he again lived the life of an exile.

From April 1902 to April 1903 Lenin and Krupskaya had lived in London, which had the great advantage that the police were not fussy about identification documents. As Herr and Frau Richter they were able to live undisturbed in two unfurnished rooms at No. 30 Holford Square, off King's Cross Road. Mrs Yeo, the landlady, did indeed interest herself in Krupskaya's failure to wear a wedding ring, but she was silenced by an oblique reference to the law of libel: and as foreigners went the Richters were tolerably respectable lodgers.

Lenin and Krupskaya had known enough English to translate the Webbs' *Industrial Democracy* in Siberia, but at first they could neither understand the spoken language nor make themselves understood. To teach themselves they went to meetings in Hyde Park (where they found the accent of an Irish atheist easiest to follow), to churches, music-halls and pubs: later Lenin exchanged lessons. His main occupation was editing *Iskra*, which was printed with the help of Harry Quelch and the English Social-Democrats; but he also spent much of his time in the reading-room of the British Museum, where forty years earlier Karl Marx had sat day after day collecting material for *Das Kapital*. Other museums bored Lenin, but he explored London thoroughly. A favourite expedition was to Marx's grave in Highgate Cemetery, then to Primrose Hill for the view over London, and back by Regent's Park and the zoo. He also loved long rides on the top of omnibuses, not only to see the sights of London, but also to observe the contrasts of wealth and poverty. Disraeli's phrase 'Two Nations' was often on his lips; and when he took Trotsky round London he said with studied carelessness as he indicated the Abbey: 'Yes, that's their Westminster.'

Lenin's last visit to London was in 1907, for a party congress which was held in the Brotherhood Church, Southgate Road. Gorky draws a vivid picture of 'the bare walls of a wooden church ... unadorned to the point of absurdity,' and Lenin in the pulpit hammering the hostile Menshevik section of the audience. It was during this congress, when the party found itself in serious financial difficulties, that George Lansbury helped Lenin to obtain a substantial loan from Mr Fels, a wealthy manufacturer. When this loan fell due on 1 January 1908, there were still no funds; and the debt was not finally honoured until after the victory of the Bolsheviks in the October Revolution. In 1923 the sum borrowed, plus accumulated interest, was repaid in full.

These financial straits were symptomatic of depression and disintegration during the years of reaction after the defeat of the revolution of 1905. It was a period of intellectual confusion and regrouping among the émigrés. Lenin characteristically devoted himself to the study of philosophy, with the object of confuting tendencies towards idealism* and religion which had arisen among some of the disillusioned socialists in exile. The result of this work was a large volume, *Materialism and Empirio-Criticism*, published in the spring of 1909, together with a mass of articles and critical writings. No more was heard of the efforts of his opponents to introduce a rival philosophy into the party.

Simultaneously Lenin was taking an active part both in the slow rebuilding of the Social-Democratic party in Russia and in the international socialist movement. On the outbreak of war in 1914 he was arrested in Austrian Galicia as a Russian spy. He was elected prisoners' representative by the inmates of the Novy Targ prison, and was finally liberated after Austrian Social-Democrats had explained that he was no friend to the tsar. Lenin retired to Switzerland, whence he fiercely attacked those socialists of all countries, and particularly Russia, who supported the war. For a time this virtually isolated him among

---

*Lenin, following Berkeley, defined idealism in the philosophic sense as the doctrine which 'claims that objects do not exist "without the mind"; objects are "combinations of sensations".' To philosophical idealism Lenin opposed materialism, with its 'recognition of "objects in themselves" or outside the mind; ideas and sensations are copies and images of these objects'.

the émigrés; but this very isolation increased his prestige as the disillusion inside Russia grew. Lenin knew from the start that the war gave the Russian Revolution its chance, and he redoubled his party activity.

2

So when he returned to Russia in April 1917, six weeks after the February Revolution, Lenin was the acknowledged head of the Bolshevik party. He had succeeded, where almost all the other exiles had failed, in keeping in close touch with developments inside his own country. For years he had carried on a steady correspondence with Russia, writing on an average ten letters a day. He devoured all information that came thence, and at once closely cross-examined any new arrival. He continually bombarded the underground party leaders inside Russia with requests for further information, as well as with advice, suggestions and protests. In 1912, for instance, when the first legal Bolshevik newspaper, *Pravda*, began to appear in St Petersburg, Lenin demanded detailed reports on the money subscribed to the paper: he wanted to know where regular subscriptions, and therefore steady support for the party, were coming from. He himself dealt personally with arrangements for smuggling letters, illegal literature and weapons into Russia.

As a result of this continuous exhausting work Lenin came to know the Russian revolutionary movements, its personnel and problems, inside out. He was the very reverse of an abstract theoretician or an out-of-touch émigré. All those who met him remarked on his very un-Russian ability to *listen*, to hear all sides to a disputed point before making up his own mind firmly and decisively. This proved especially valuable after the Bolshevik Revolution, when Lenin was Chairman of the Council of People's Commissars. In this post his final summing-up would often synthesize clashing views in a way which would convince their advocates. This attentive and receptive chairmanship, this deliberation before reaching the ultimate decision, did not preclude firmness and indeed ruthlessness when his mind was made up, as we shall frequently have occasion to see. All these qualities explain why, on his return to Russia in 1905 and 1917, Lenin was able at once to assume the lead of the party, and in the latter year actually to change its policy. Outside observers found this difficult to understand, and spoke of 'dictatorship', or (in 1917) of 'German gold'. The secret lay, however, in the hard detailed work to which Lenin had devoted himself during the years of preparation. His Menshevik opponent Dan said of him: 'There is no one else who for the whole twenty-four hours of every day is busy with the revolution, who thinks and even dreams only of the revolution. What can you do with a man like that?'

Lenin was very highly strung, and his political quarrels with personal friends cost him a great deal. He himself graphically described the bitterness of disillusion which his first dispute with Plekhanov caused him. During the party controversies of 1903 Lenin was accused by his enemies of being an 'autocrat' in discussion, and he himself admitted to being excitable. But by 1917 he had matured. His wife, looking back to the nine years of their second exile, describes Lenin's complete absorption in the political cause to which he had dedicated himself:

He would break off relations wth his closest friends if he thought they were hampering the movement; and he could approach an opponent of yesterday in a simple and comradely way if the cause required it. He was as blunt and straightforward as ever. He loved the country, the verdant forests, the mountain paths, and lakes; but he also loved the noise of a big city, and crowds of workers, his comrades, the movement, the struggle, life with all its facets. However, watching him closely from day to day, one could observe that he became more reserved, more considerate of people, and more reflective. The years of exile were hard to bear and drained much of Lenin's strength. But they made him the fighter the másses needed and the one who led them to victory.

At the beginning of 1917 Lenin and Krupskaya were living at No. 14 Spiegelgasse, Zürich, paying twenty-eight francs a month for a second-floor bed-sitting-room, with use of kitchen. On 8

April Lenin told his landlord that they must leave at once, although the rent was paid until the end of the month. Herr Kammerer wished him luck, and said: 'I hope, Herr Ulyanov, that in Russia you won't have to work so hard as here.' Lenin answered thoughtfully: 'I think, Herr Kammerer, that in Petrograd I shall have even more work.' Two hours later he was in the train which took him and thirty-two other revolutionaries through Germany to Sweden and Russia. On the day of his arrival in Petrograd the Ministry of Foreign Affairs received a memorandum from the British Embassy in which Lenin was described as an extremely dangerous man, but a good organizer, who was 'very likely' to find numerous followers in the capital.

Part Two
The Revolution

3   A Party of a New Type

> 'In its struggle for power the proletariat has no other weapon but organization.' (LENIN *in* 1904)

I

Three months before Lenin was born Karl Marx settled down to a serious study of the Russian language and Russian economic conditions. Russian was the first language into which *Das Kapital* was translated – in 1872; and its success in Russia was great and immediate. The field had been prepared for Marxism by the materialism of Belinsky and Chernishevsky in the middle of the nineteenth century; and subsequently the rapid industrial development of the country created a favourable intellectual atmosphere. By 1890 there were factories employing two and a half million workers in Russia.

On the basis of a searching historical and economic analysis, Marx argued that just as feudalism had been violently overthrown and replaced by capitalism, so the capitalist order itself would be overthrown and give way to socialism. He regarded this as inevitable, not only because of the inherent tendency to breakdown in capitalist economy, but also because in its expansion capitalism itself produced 'its own grave-diggers', in the shape of the proletariat, the class which was to succeed to its inheritance. Their economic situation impressed upon the working class the need for united struggle against their employers, and so they came by experience to appreciate the value of organized and disciplined cooperation. The conditions of their life made them potential socialists, just as the employers were naturally individualists, competing against each other as well as enriching themselves at the expense of their employees. A rational organization of society with the object of producing and equitably distributing the maximum of wealth would be possible only when the anarchy of production for private profit had been abolished, and the means of production taken over by the working class themselves. But history, Marx held, taught that no possessing class would ever go quietly; just as political power had to be violently seized by the bourgeoisie in its time, so a revolution would also be necessary to transfer power from the bourgeoisie to the proletariat.

The attractions of a part of this theory for Russia in the closing decades of the nineteenth century are obvious. Marx carefully and fully analysed the tasks of the 'bourgeois revolution', and emphasized the historical progressiveness of the capitalist in contrast to the feudal order. At a time when the Slavophils were glorifying the Russian brand of feudalism as a unique historical phenomenon which must be preserved at all costs, Marx's complete contempt for any survival of feudalism as an anachronism in the nineteenth century won the assent of many intellectuals who had no desire to see anything more advanced than a liberal parliamentary régime in Russia, and who at that time had no fear of those who were to prove the 'gravediggers' of capitalism in Russia. 'Nearly everyone became a Marxist,' as Lenin put it scornfully in 1902.

The first Russian Marxist circle, an offshoot from the Narodniks, was the Emancipation of Labour Group, founded in 1883, whose most prominent figure was Plekhanov. Even before the assassination of Alexander II had failed to produce either the expected peasant revolt or concessions from the autocracy, this group of exiles decided that terrorism was ineffective for their purposes. They transferred their hopes of revolution from the peasantry to the new town working class. When Lenin went abroad in 1895 it was with the Emancipation of Labour Group in Switzerland that he made contact. By this date, thanks largely to the propaganda work of Plekhanov, a Marxist school of thought had differentiated itself from the Narodniks. But Plekhanov's group had hitherto occupied themselves with translations of the works of Marx and Engels, and with theoretical writings aimed at the educated classes. There was as yet no

Russian political party which identified itself with the theory of Marxism and tried to broadcast that theory among the masses of the population. To the establishment of such a party Lenin contributed more than any other single individual.

In analysing the position which the Russian Marxists took up against the Narodniks, and which subsequently was adopted as the platform of the Russian Social-Democratic party, I shall draw largely on Lenin's writings, since it was Lenin who publicized, organized and thought out tactics. But the germ of many of the ideas which Lenin developed against the Narodniks he owed, as he would have been the first to admit, to Plekhanov. Plekhanov was a man of keen critical intellect and biting wit, with a most attractive prose style. His approach to political questions was sometimes academic, and he later proved to be quite ineffectual in the rough-and-tumble of a real revolution. But despite all their later controversies, Lenin always retained affection and admiration for one who had so valuable an iconoclastic influence on the generation which grew up in the eighties and nineties. Gorky captured the different psychologies of the two men when he wrote: 'I have rarely met two people with less in common than G. V. Plekhanov and V. I. Lenin. ... The one was finishing his work of destroying the old world, the other was beginning the construction of a new.'

2

The Narodniks regarded Russian capitalism as an 'artificial' creation, introduced from the West, and alien to the whole Russian tradition. Lenin had no difficulty in showing that capitalism was developing spontaneously, and argued that in feudal Russia capitalism was a progressive phenomenon. His main argument against the Narodniks was that with the development of capitalism (and consequently of an urban working class) in Russia the possibility of a socialist revolution had emerged. To advocate 'Russian socialism' on the basis of the peasant commune (as the early Narodniks did) was now to play into the hands of reaction: capitalism had developed to such an extent in Russia, even in the countryside, that rich peasants dominated the commune, and a transition to socialism was possible only by a revolution against both tsarism and the bourgeoisie, including the rich peasantry. Consequently it was time for socialists to cut themselves loose from those who merely advocated the overthrow of tsarism and the granting of democratic reforms. 'Political liberty ... will not improve the conditions of the workers, but only improve the conditions for their struggle against the bourgeoisie.' Therefore, Lenin argued, those who advocated a peasant revolt must decide whether they wished such a revolt to take place under the leadership of the middle-class liberals or under the leadership of the working class. The idea that the peasantry as a homogeneous social group could play an independent role in the impending revolution was nonsensical, for the peasantry was already sharply divided into rich and poor: the interests of the former were indistinguishable from those of the middle class, whilst the poor peasantry had common enemies with the working class.

In contrast to the Narodnik thesis that 'the man of the future' was the peasant, Lenin argued that 'the Russian worker is the sole and natural representative of the whole of the labouring and exploited population of Russia. He is the natural representative because, *by its very nature*, the exploitation of the workers in Russia *is everywhere capitalist*, if we leave out of account the moribund remnants of serf economy.' 'It is not only the injustice of indvidual officials that the worker has to contend with, but the injustice of the state, which protects the whole of the capitalist class. ... Thus the fight between the factory workers and the factory owner inevitably becomes a fight against the whole capitalist class, against the whole social system based on the exploitation of labour by capital.' 'The working class ... *alone* is the truly consistent and unreserved enemy of absolutism, it is *only* between the working class and absolutism that compromise is impossible. ... The hostility of all other classes, groups and strata of the population towards the autocracy is not absolute; their democracy always looks back.'

Hence the working class should become the leader in the struggle of all the discontented elements of society against absolutism, should not follow behind the liberal parties as a 'ginger group'. (Here the argument turns against the 'reformist' wing of the Social-Democratic party, those who were to be known as the Mensheviks.) Taking into account the behaviour of European liberals in the nineteenth century, Lenin argued that from the nature of their position in society the Russian liberal bourgeoisie as a class, together with the liberal intelligentsia, could never be more than half-hearted revolutionaries, that they would sell out to tsarism as soon as they had attained their minimum objectives. 'We must take upon ourselves the task of organizing a universal political struggle under the leadership of *our party* in such a manner as to obtain all possible support from all opposition strata for the struggle and for our party.' 'The party ... must learn to catch every liberal just at the moment when he is prepared to move forward an inch, and force him to go forward a yard. If he is obstinate and won't – we shall go forward without him and over his body.'

Against those who wished the Social-Democrats to confine themselves to trade-union matters, to the immediate improvement of the everyday life of the workers, Lenin replied: 'The aim of bourgeois policy is to assist the economic struggle of the proletariat; the aim of the socialist is to compel the economic struggle to aid the socialist movement and contribute to the success of the revolutionary workers' party.' 'The social democrat's ideal should not be a trade-union secretary but a *tribune of the people*, able to react to every manifestation of tyranny and oppression, no matter where it takes place, no matter what stratum or class of the people it affects; he must be able to group all these manifestations into a single picture of police violence and capitalist exploitation.'

3

Before Lenin's exile to Siberia, the St Petersburg League of Struggle was working towards the foundation of a Russian

Social-Democratic party. Such a party was actually established in 1898, but most of the leaders were arrested almost immediately after the foundation congress. When Lenin returned from exile the party had ceased to exist as an effective organization. Moreover, different trends had by that time emerged among the Marxists: it was to try to clear up these disagreements and to publicize his own conception of what the theory and practice of a Marxist party should be that Lenin went abroad to cooperate with Plekhanov and other émigrés in founding the newpaper *Iskra*. Since all was to do again, he was determined that this time it should be done thoroughly.

At that stage Lenin regarded the creation of a Social-Democratic newspaper as all-important for two reasons, ideological and organizational. 'It is necessary to bring about unity of ideas which will remove the differences of opinion and confusion that – we will be frank – reign among Russian Social-Democrats at the present time. Unity of ideas must be fortified by means of a party programme.' Otherwise intellectual effort would merely be squandered in provincial controversies and struggles. In these circumstances the Social-Democrats could not be such 'tribunes of the people' as Lenin wished to see, leading all classes of society in the struggle against autocracy. *Iskra*'s two-way underground mailing system – supplying information from Russia to the editors, and sending back *Iskra* and its subsidiary publications – was the best practical method of uniting the scattered centres. Personnel were trained 'who will devote to the revolution not only their spare evenings but the whole of their lives,' and were given definite jobs to do as part of a programme of conspiratorial activity: so the dissipation of physical effort was prevented and the shattered party was restored. And now Lenin was at the very centre of the Russian Social-Democratic organization. In 1903 it was decided that the time was ripe for the calling of a new party congress; *Iskra*'s agents did almost all the preparatory work.

4

Lenin was anxious to tighten up the organization and thought of the party in opposition to certain developments in the international socialist movement, which, he considered, were unduly influencing a number of Russian émigrés.

The Russian Social-Democratic party founded in 1898 was a member of the Socialist (Second) International, established nine years earlier to unite all socialist parties (and trade unions) which recognized the class struggle.* The international solidarity of the working-class movement was one of the first precepts of these parties. The dominant party in the Second International was the German Social-Democratic party. It was the strongest numerically; it had the largest parliamentary representation; Germany was the homeland of Marxism, and German theoreticians – Kautsky, Bernstein – were the most influential in the international socialist movement. The average Russian political émigré held the German Social-Democratic leaders in great reverence when he first went abroad, and had no higher ambition than to sit at their feet.

But the more penetrating eye of Lenin detected something rotten in the state of the German party. He already observed the weaknesses which were ultimately to lead to that day in August 1914 when the parliamentary elders of the great German Social-Democratic party voted war credits to the Kaiser's government, in defiance of their solemnly professed obligations. The same treachery, as Lenin considered it, was shown by almost all the leaders of the socialist parties of the great European powers as they became involved in the war. He believed, then and much earlier, that the rapid numerical expansion of the German and other parties had been accompanied by a progressive debasement of Marxist theory rather than by an education of the membership up to the theory.

These parties, he argued, were becoming too concerned with

---

*The First International, founded by Marx in 1864, had come to an end soon after the defeat of the Paris Commune in 1871.

details of trade-union and parliamentary politics, with winning economic concessions and votes, and were relegating their socialist objectives to an ever-receding future. The leaders were acquiring a vested interest in well-paid official posts in the party and trade-union hierarchy, whose existence depended on the maintenance of the capitalist system. They were becoming psychologically adapted to making that system work, and found it easier to extract concessions for their rank and file when it worked profitably. Thus the bureaucratic leaders were able to rely on the political backwardness of rank-and-file democracy to slur over the contrast between their revolutionary phrases and their compromising practice. Some of the German leaders, notably Bernstein, openly advocated a revision of the official Marxism of the party, so as to remove the revolutionary planks from its platform. Others, such as Kautsky, continued to do lip service to orthodoxy, but in 1914 adopted a position which differed only verbally from that of the 'revisionists'.

Already from Siberia Lenin had thundered against Bernstein and his Russian imitators, and he was determined that the Russian party should not go the same way as the German. *Iskra* was created to oppose a 'revisionist' journal, *Rabocheye Delo,* and Lenin intended that his paper should help not only to keep the principles of Russian Social-Democracy pure, but also to build up the form of party organization which he thought essential for Russia. By 1903 he hoped that these objects had been achieved.

5

Lenin's idea of party organization was so different from that which had hitherto been normal in western Europe that it is worth recalling that he was developing the Russian revolutionary tradition. In order to control a rebellious and evasive peasantry all over the vast Russian spaces an absolute, highly centralized and bureaucratic government had come into existence. The autocracy conditioned the movements which stood out against it. Opposition was necessarily revolutionary. This was so whether it took the form of the wild peasant revolt of Pugachov or of the Guards' palace revolutions, which in the eighteenth century made and unmade tsars, until the aristocratic conspiracy of the Decembrists in 1825 brought old and new together – the last Guards' revolt (and the first to be unsuccessful) and the first revolutionary movement influenced by the liberal ideas of the West. As control by the police inside Russia tightened, so the opposition movements became increasingly conspiratorial. Among the Decembrists Pestel advocated the formation of small underground groups united by a common revolutionary purpose. In the seventies and eighties Tkachev carried this further by calling for a centralized and disciplined body of professional revolutionaries. Such a body existed for a few years in the Land and Liberty Group (*Zemlya i Volya*), and its successor, the Party of People's Will (*Narodnaya Volya*), whose programmes, adopted in 1879, provided for 'the organization of secret societies to be coordinated under a central headquarters'.

There was thus a constant theme in Russian revolutionary politics – the demand for a closely-knit federation of conspiratorial groups, united by a single will. This principle of conservation of energy sharply distinguished the professional revolutionaries from the liberal intellectuals and the early Narodniks who 'went to the people' and exhausted their strength in futile struggle against the hydra-headed bureaucracy: what they most conspicuously lacked was unity of purpose and coordination of action.

The autocracy had a single and ruthless will: there was no room for controversy and disagreement among the revolutionaries trying to overthrow it. The *Narodnaya Volya* party had been a small and devoted band of terrorists; but the failure of the assassination of Alexander II to produce anything but negative results showed that tsarism could outlive the tsar. The revolutionary groups split up, and many turned to the ideas and principles of organization of Western Social-Democracy. Lenin, however, always highly valued the courage, audacity and complete self-abnegation of the early terrorists, for whom the revolution was the one thing in life. He set this heroic tradition in opposition to the rather humdrum parliamentarism of German Social-Democracy.

The Russian Social-Democrats discarded terrorism, on the ground that it was an obstacle to the development of a mass workers' movement. But – thanks largely to Lenin – the Bolsheviks absorbed much of the specifically Russian tradition of revolutionary organization. The secret groups, so essential for underground work against autocracy, were welded into a party united by a common theory. This party was regarded as the nucleus around which a mass workers' movement could be built up. The Bolshevik party far surpassed the tsarist bureaucracy in unity of purpose, conviction, devotion to duty and discipline. It was not for nothing that Lenin fought against the older theoreticians of the Social-Democratic party for a leading nucleus of 'experienced revolutionaries, no less professionally trained than the police'. Is it possible in Russia, he asked, 'for all the revolutionaries to elect one of their members to office when, in the very interests of the work, he *must* conceal his identity from nine out of ten of these "all"? . . . The only serious organizational principle the active workers of our movement can accept is strict secrecy, strict selection of members, and the training of professional revolutionaries.'

6

The party congress of 1903 did not prove to be the walk-over which Lenin had perhaps expected. Exponents of the west European type of Social-Democratic party appeared on behalf of émigré groups represented at the congress, and received unexpected support from some of those who had hitherto cooperated with Plekhanov and Lenin in editing *Iskra*. The issue was thrashed out in a discussion over point No. 1 of the party rules. Lenin and those later known as Bolsheviks wished to restrict membership to those who recognized the party's programme and 'personally participate in one of the organizations of the party'. For this clause Martov and those later known as Mensheviks succeeded in substituting 'work under the control and guidance of one of the organizations of the party'. Behind what seemed at the time a comparatively minor disagreement Lenin came to see two entirely different conceptions of party organization in conflict.

In underground work, Lenin argued, 'it is almost impossible for us to distinguish talkers from workers. And there is hardly another country in the world in which confusion of these two categories is as common, causes such enormous muddle and does so much damage as in Russia. We suffer severely from the presence of this evil, not only among the intelligentsia, but also in the ranks of the working class, and Comrade Martov's formula legalizes it. . . . It is better that ten who actually work should not call themselves members of the party (real workers don't hunt for titles!) than that one talker should have the right and opportunity to be a party member.'

The Mensheviks were thinking in terms of a parliamentary party which would appeal to the maximum number of the electorate by making the minimum demands on members; but in Russia in 1903 there was neither parliament nor electorate. Lenin argued that blind advocacy of a Western type of party under Russian conditions was aimed at attracting the support of 'professors and university students', who would never submit to the discipline necessary for successful underground work. The Bolsheviks aimed at creating 'a party of a new type', whose members should be united by complete understanding of an agreement on their fundamental objectives, and all of whom would be ready to work for their achievement, under orders where necessary. 'Little and good', 'make smaller to make greater' were Lenin's slogans on this and many subsequent occasions. A Western parliamentary party would be the sum of a number of separate individuals, not an organism with a single will: it would correspond to the atomic structure of bourgeois society, not to the factory whose discipline and organization 'based on collective work organized under conditions of technically highly developed production' Lenin recommended as a model for middle-class intellectuals. The working class is 'trained for organization by its whole life', in a way that the gentlemen anarchists who preponderated among the émigrés could never understand.

Marxism is a product of the West. Marx and Engels evolved their theory on the basis of an analysis of the industrial civilization about them, drawing, as Lenin put it, on the heritage of German philosophy, English political economy and French political thought. It is one of the paradoxes of the Russian Revolution that this theory, rejected by the leaders of the largest socialist parties of the West, should be adopted by a revolutionary group whose native traditions were so different from those of parliamentary democracy.

This is what makes the conflict between Bolsheviks and Mensheviks in 1903 far more than a clash between two views of organization and of tactics; and here we sense something of Lenin's greatness. Consider his own words on the ripeness of revolutionary Russia for Marxism:

> For almost half a century – roughly from the forties to the nineties of the last century – advanced thinkers in Russia, under the oppression of an unprecedented, savage and reactionary tsarism, sought eagerly for the correct revolutionary theory and followed each and every 'last word' in Europe and America in this sphere with astonishing diligence and thoroughness. Russia achieved Marxism, the only correct revolutionary theory, virtually through *suffering*, by half a century ... of unprecedented revolutionary heroism, incredible energy, devoted searching, study, testing in practice, disappointments, checking and comparison with European experience.

Lenin made his life-work the application of Marxism to the specific conditions of Russia. In him two worlds met: the native revolutionary tradition, springing from the necessities of Russian life and shaped by the structure of the tsarist state, was modified by the scientific socialism, the careful analysis of the class forces in a given situation, which Lenin derived from Marxism. Neither of the two traditions which met in Lenin and to which the Bolsheviks gave expression in 1903 – that of the Russian revolutionaries and that of Marxism – had much in common with the liberal parliamentary tradition which the Mensheviks wanted to transplant to the unsuitable soil of Russia. The Social-Democracy of Bernstein and the German 're-visionists' was as out of place in Russia as the English liberalism of Struve: it had no social roots. Although Mensheviks preponderated abroad, the local committees of the party in Russia were mainly Bolshevik. So were the principal trade unions. 'The Leninists ... have behind them in Russia an overwhelming majority of the underground social-democratic organizations,' it was noted in the Police Department during the war.

For these reasons, as soon as it came to the test of practice, Bolshevism – till then one of many factions, not on the surface conspicuously stronger than Menshevism – swept all before it. When Lenin spoke to the crowd outside the Finland station from his armoured car in April 1917, there spoke in him, not merely the disciple of Marx and Engels, but also the heir of Pestel, Chernishevsky and Zhelyabov: as Lenin himself very well knew. The epigraph of *Iskra* ('The Spark') was a phrase used in a letter from a group of Decembrist exiles in Siberia to Pushkin: 'A spark will kindle a flame.'

7

There was, however, a real dilemma in combining socialism and discipline in the party. Lenin recognized that 'in Russia the theory of Social Democracy arose quite independently of the spontaneous growth of the labour movement; it arose as a natural and inevitable outcome of the development of ideas among the revolutionary socialist intelligentsia.' Marxism could only be brought into the labour movement 'from without' since only intellectuals of the well-to-do classes had the education, leisure and facilities for theoretical study. And 'without a revolutionary theory there can be no revolutionary movement.'

There was the problem. All Russian revolutionary movements in the nineteenth century had been dominated by intellectuals. But as the century advanced the intelligentsia, drawn mostly from the propertied classes, yet rejecting the social system which maintained them, lost their own roots and stability. Russian novels of this period have made proverbial the general fecklessness, indecision and 'dressing-gown mentality' of the pre-revolutionary intelligentsia.

Lenin was always suspicious of his own class, arguing that intellectuals were inevitably affected by the capitalist development of Russia and the new possibilities of comfortable and lucrative employment which were offered them if they would abandon the revolutionary theories of an earlier age. Accordingly he strove to ensure that a high proportion of workers occupied leading party posts. Intellectuals necessarily predominated among the theoreticians and organizers abroad; but Lenin continually jeered at and warned against those who lost touch with the revolutionary movement in Russia. In 1915 he declared: 'Half a century of Russian political emigration (and thirty years of *Social-Democratic* organization) have ... proved that all declarations, conferences, etc., abroad are powerless, unimportant, fictitious, if they are not supported by a lasting movement of a definite social stratum in Russia.' In 1917 two thirds of the members of the party were workers.

The solution then, as Lenin saw it, was for the workers in the party to maintain control over their leaders while utilizing their theoretical knowledge and training new leaders who would have assimilated the teachings of the theorists. Meanwhile intellectuals must realize their role and their limitations; they must not use the theoretical 'backwardness' of the workers as an excuse for not leading them forward, must not, in the words of Plekhanov, 'gaze with awe upon the backsides of the Russian proletariat' .'The intellectuals', said Lenin, 'must talk to us less of what we already know and tell us more about what we do not know and what we can never learn from our factory and trade-union experience.' Once 'a real party is formed [i.e. after 1903], the class-conscious worker must learn to distinguish the mentality of the soldier of the proletarian army from the mentality of the bourgeois intellectual who flaunts anarchist phrases; he must learn to *insist* that the duties of a party member be fulfilled not only by the rank and file, but by the "people at the top" as well.'

This last remark was directed at the Menshevik leaders. Although they secured the adoption of their version of No. 1 of the rules at the beginning of the 1903 congress, the subsequent withdrawal of a right-wing group left a stable Bolshevik majority. (Henceforth only is it accurate to speak of the two groups as Bolshevik and Menshevik, the names being derived from the Russian words for majority and minority respectively.) The Mensheviks refused to accept many of the decisions of the majority, and from this time onwards, although the two factions occasionally cooperated, they were in effect two separate parties. Formal separation finally took place in 1912.

8

It has seemed worth while dwelling on this early and apparently trivial disagreement because of the real difference of outlook bound up with the dispute about party organization. This was made clear in action during the revolution of 1905, when the Mensheviks argued that, in a bourgeois revolution, the main driving force must be the liberals, and that the Social-Democrats should merely help the liberal parties to win constitutional reforms, whilst doing nothing to frighten them into reaction. The Bolsheviks had inherited from Marx and Engels the conception that even the bourgeois-democratic revolution would not be completed by the bourgeoisie without much pushing and shoving from the 'plebeian elements' in society: Lenin and his supporters consequently wished to give an independent lead, and to call out the peasantry as allies.

Events were soon to justify these tactics. Although a constitution was granted in 1906, within less than two years the franchise had been so narrowed that a single landed proprietor had as much share in the election of deputies to the State Duma as over five hundred urban workers. There was thus no prospect of the working-class parties winning power that way; and indeed the functions of the Duma were so circumscribed that a revolution was necessary before even the liberal parties could come to power in March 1917.

After this revolution the Mensheviks first supported the Cadet government, then joined in a coalition with the Cadets and the Socialist Revolutionaries to continue the war against Germany; the Bolsheviks opposed both the government and the war and led the second revolution of October 1917, by which the Mensheviks were thrust aside. In January 1918 the representatives of the latter were still repeating plaintively that this was a bourgeois revolution and that 'all possible social attainments of the working masses are not capable of changing the foundations of the capitalist order'; consequently 'socialist experiments' would lead merely to economic disintegration. After this grandiose confession of political bankruptcy the leaders of the Menshevik party disappeared from history as the coadjutors of the White Guards, trying with the aid of foreign bayonets to demonstrate the impossibility of the socialist experiments of the Bolsheviks.

Whether or not one accepts Lenin's dictum that 'Bolshevism can serve as a model of tactics for all,' there can be no doubt that, given the necessity of revolution for the attainment of even modest reforms, the Bolshevik conception of the party was far better suited to Russian conditions than the Menshevik copy of Western models which in very different conditions had adapted themselves to a non-revolutionary struggle. Lenin afterwards declared that the years between 1903 and 1917 were years of practical experience in applying Marxism to Russian conditions, years which

in wealth of experience had no equal anywhere else in the world. For no other country during these fifteen years had anything even approximating to this revolutionary experience, this rapid and varied succession of different forms of the movement — legal and illegal, peaceful and stormy, underground and open, small circles and mass movements, parliamentary and terrorist. In no other country was there concentrated during so short a period of time such a wealth of forms, shades and methods of struggle involving *all* classes of modern society, and, moreover, of a struggle which, owing to the backwardness of the country and the heavy yoke of tsarism, matured with exceptional rapidity and assimilated most eagerly the appropriate 'last word' of American and European political experience.

That in these years of trial the Bolsheviks had evolved a political philosophy and analysis of events more realistic than those of any of their rivals was shown by the ease with which they swept aside all other parties in the revolutionary months of 1917. In Germany after November 1918, in not dissimilar conditions of military defeat and social revolution, the great German Social-Democratic party, with its millions of members, proved incapable of sizing up the situation and producing an agreed and positive revolutionary policy.

In Russia in 1917 it was Bolshevik mastery of the *fact* that was decisive. The party knew exactly what it wanted, what *concrete* concessions to make to different social groups at any given stage, how to convince the masses of the population by *actions*, its own and their own. The party's organization allowed great flexibility in manoeuvre, combined with firmness and strength in pursuit of the clearly envisaged ultimate objective. It was this which won the confidence of a following sufficient to enable the Bolsheviks to seize and retain power whilst the Mensheviks and Socialist Revolutionaries discredited themselves by the helplessness of their most eloquent phrases in face of the rude and stubborn fact.

After the October Revolution and the civil war the Communist party (Bolsheviks), already so different in structure and principles from the west European Social-Democratic parties, became the only legal political organization in the state, something hardly recognizable as a party at all: a 'vocation of leadership' the Webbs have called it. Joining the party was made very difficult; Lenin insisted on a long period of probation and frequent purges with the object of preventing an influx of time-servers and careerists once the natural selection of underground work had ceased to operate. Having been accepted, it was not easy to remain a member unless one justified oneself by works as well as by faith. The party was thought of as a body of highly-trained, disinterested and energetic persons, capable of planning the construction of socialism and convincing the uneducated mass of their compatriots. Admission to this body was not lightly to be earned. But on two occasions the doors of the party were thrown wide open. The first was in August 1919, the blackest moment of the war of intervention, when Denikin's army was directly threatening Moscow; and 120,000 new members joined the party. After Lenin's death in 1924 there was an even larger mass enrolment. 'In those days of mourning', says the official *History of the Communist Party of the Soviet Union,* 'every class-conscious worker defined his attitude to the Communist Party', and 240,000 new members joined it, pledging themselves to carry on Lenin's work.

4 Towards a Workers' and Peasants' State

'On your decisions, on the decisions of the majority of the people, will depend the ultimate fate of our country.' (LENIN – *Draft address to the rural population, December 1917*)

I

It is a familiar paradox that the revolution which the Bolsheviks describe as 'proletarian' took place in a country where eighty per cent of the inhabitants were peasants, and where the proletariat was smaller, both relatively and absolutely, than in any other great European power. The object of this chapter is to consider how Bolshevik policy solved this apparent contradiction.

There could be no doubt about the revolutionary potentialities of the Russian peasantry if a correct political approach to them could be found. There was a tradition in the Russian villages, as indeed there had been in all European countries under serfdom, that the land belonged by right to the peasants. This was based partly on recollections of the freer social order which had preceded serfdom, partly on the obvious claim in equity of those who cultivated the soil to consume its fruits. In 1861 serfdom was abolished. The land in the villages was divided roughly into two halves: one half was given to the peasant inhabitants (not in full ownership), the other to the lords. As a result the peasants possessed less land than they had actually cultivated hitherto.

For the allotments granted to them the peasants had to pay an annual redemption charge to the government, which had already compensated the landlords. This redemption charge, insultingly but significantly, was given the name formerly used for the serf's commutation fee. Until the total 'allotment price' was paid off the peasant remained liable to certain feudal servitudes. The 'allotment price' was assessed very high, whilst the peasant normally found the worst land allotted to him: the landlord usually acquired all the forest lands from which the peasant had hitherto obtained his fuel and timber. All but the richest peasants ran hopelessly into debt in the attempt to meet these annual payments, until they were finally abolished as a result of the revolution of 1905. It was calculated when the redemption payments came to an end that the value of the lands allotted to the peasantry in 1861 had already been paid three times over. Lenin approvingly quoted the radical publicist Chernishevsky, who wrote at a time when most Russian liberals were taken in by the 'great reform': 'Those peasants who have money will buy land. What's the use of compelling the peasants who have no money to buy land? It will only ruin them. Buying out in instalments is buying just the same.' 'There is no freedom without land,' Herzen had insisted in 1865.

Between 1861 and 1905 the average size of peasants' holdings diminished by one third. This tendency was accelerated by the growth of population, itself due in part to the improved medical services which the Zemstvo liberals had introduced. In the meantime possession of his inadequate allotment and the difficulty of obtaining a passport tied the peasant to the soil as effectively as he had ever been tied by feudal custom; and so a pool of cheap labour was available for the landlord. Agrarian overpopulation was estimated at 20 millions before the revolution – i.e. nearly one in every five of the rural inhabitants was economically superfluous. From 1886 the landlord had the right to dismiss his labourers without notice – for 'rudeness', among other things; the labourer had no right to break his contract even on grounds of ill-treatment: if he fled, the police brought him back. From 1906 it was a penal offence for agricultural labourers to strike.

'Although the peasants paid for the liberation,' wrote Lenin, 'they did not become free men; for twenty years they remained "temporarily bonded"; they were left and have remained to this day [April 1901] the lower estate, who could be flogged, who paid special taxes, who had no right freely to leave the semi-feudal commune, freely to dispose of their own land or to settle freely in any part of the state.' The poll tax, totalling 42 million roubles a year, was levied exclusively on the peasants; and of the remaining 166 million roubles direct taxation, they paid 153 million. One of Turgenev's 'Prose Poems' is about a peasant cab-driver who was forced to come to town for a time in order to earn money to pay his taxes: during his absence his wife died of cholera. 'The peasant', said Lenin, 'had to obtain money at all costs in order to pay the taxes which had been heaped up as a result of the "beneficial reform", in order to lease land, in order to buy a few miserable manufactured goods – which were beginning to squeeze out the domestic manufactures of the peasant – to buy bread, etc.'

The peasant thus became increasingly conscious of the state as an alien and hostile force, which made demands without conferring benefits. This attitude had its effect on the development of the Russian peasant parties, in whose policies there was a considerable element of anarchism. The peasant did not, however, wholly transfer his hostility from the landlord to the state. If one of his main objectives was to free himself from the crushing annuity payments on his share of the land, another was to seize the remainder. The settlement of 1861 had made the unequal relationship of peasant to lord geographically obvious. The former looked upon the enclosures round the lord's land as an artificial obstacle arbitrarily set up, which he was determined to pull down at the first opportunity. For the peasantry the revolution of 1905 was 'the levelling'.

The 'emancipation' in the long run increased the uneasiness of the gentry – partly because it thus stimulated feelings of class hostility among the peasantry, partly too because it made their own position as parasites in society overwhelmingly clear. Many landlords were absentees, whose lands were cultivated by peasant labour differing from serf labour only in that the labourers were paid wages. It was this feeling of guilt, of occupying a position of exploitation unparalleled in the Western world to which they looked for culture and ideas, that by the beginning of the twentieth century had deprived any thinking landlord of confidence in the social system which maintained him. Yet the intellectuals of the Russian landed class were equally critical of social relations as they had developed in the West. In *Anna Karenina*, published in 1877, Levin was feeling for 'some relation with labour' which would avoid the capitalist system in agriculture, with which the rest of Europe was dissatisfied. Many of the early Narodniks were aristocratic intellectuals like Tolstoy's hero.

It was thus no accident that Lenin's first substantial writings dealt with the Russian peasantry. The peasant was, in Turgenev's phrase, 'the sphinx of all the Russias'. All parties wished for his support, most claimed to have it, yet there was little reliable evidence of what the dark mass of the peasantry was really thinking. The Slavophils and the Narodniks romanticized over the decaying communal institutions of the Russian village, which combined self-government in the lesser affairs of agricultural life with regulation by the bureaucracy in everything that mattered. The bourgeois liberals, with one eye on western Europe, idealized the richer peasants, the kulaks. Like their predecessors in seventeenth- and eighteenth-century England, who praised the yeoman as the backbone of the country, the Russian liberals by focusing attention on the kulaks diverted it from the mass of the peasantry who were being pauperized. The early Russian Marxists, concentrating on the antithesis between bourgeoisie and proletariat, at first tended to ignore the peasantry. They directed their main propaganda to the city workers, in contrast to the Narodniks, for whom 'going to the people' meant going to the peasantry.

But there the peasants were – the vast majority of the Russian people. Under any circumstances they would be a great force. In the past they had been a revolutionary force. In 1774–6 a rising of the peasantry (together with the Urals factory workers), led by Pugachov, had won control of great areas of Russia on either side of the Volga. Before and after 1861 there had been agrarian riots, landlords' homes had been burned, enclosures pulled down. When Lenin reached maturity the conditions of the mass of the peasantry were becoming intolerable, and the countryside was seething with the discontent which was to break out almost spontaneously in 1905–7. The party which could find out how to rouse and lead the peasantry would wield the mightiest force in Russia.

2

Lenin knew a good deal about the agrarian problem at first hand. In Kazan, at the age of eighteen, he roused comment by spending hours discussing their problems with peasants. During his legal practice in Samara he specialized on land disputes and the defence of poor peasants. Even earlier he had carried on a long argument with a local radical in his mother's village as to the extent of capitalist development in the neighbourhood of Samara. Typically, Lenin set this friend to collect detailed figures from over two hundred families, on a form which he himself drew up. When he left for St Petersburg, Lenin did not cease to agitate until the completed forms were sent after him.

In the very different conditions of Siberia Lenin again gave regular legal advice to, and extracted information from, the relatively prosperous local farmers. Whilst others theorized about the village commune, speculated on the prospects of a direct transition from it to socialism, discussed the peasant soul, Lenin got hold of all the blue books and official studies which threw light on the actual position of the peasantry, and produced detailed statistical analyses. These were *The Development of Capitalism in Russia* (1899), followed by *The Agrarian Question in Russia* (1908), still the classical works on the subject.

The title of the earlier work suggests the conclusions which Lenin reached. He established that the village commune was in fact in full process of dissolution, and was being replaced by the capitalist farmer on the one hand and agricultural wage labourers on the other. He showed that it was misleading to speak of 'the peasantry' as a single social group and a single political force; in fact it was divided by conflicting class interests. Lenin distinguished three groups: (1) the rich farmers, kulaks, cultivating fifty acres and upwards, whom he calculated at twelve per cent of the rural population of Russia, holding thirty-one per cent of the land; (2) the middle peasants, small proprietors, with holdings of thirty-five to fifty acres, who formed seven per cent of the rural population and held seven per cent of the land; (3) the poor peasants, whose holdings were less than thirty-five acres, and who were normally horseless or with only one horse, frequently dependent on their earnings as wage labourers to make both ends meet: these Lenin estimated at eighty-one per cent of the rural population, holding thirty-five per cent of the land. Their numbers were increasing. There remained the big land-owners – 0.002 per cent of the rural population, who owned twenty-seven per cent of the land.

Capitalism was thus growing in the Russian countryside. But there was one retarding factor: the *mir*. '*Mir*' is a splendid Russian word which signifies not only 'village commune', but also three things which were originally synonymous with it for the peasant: 'the world', 'the universe' and 'peace'. A violator of the commune was also a breaker of the peace. This ancient institution was the scene of such democracy and self-government as existed in nineteenth-century Russia. The commune owned the villagers' lands, although they were normally cultivated separately: from time to time it redistributed the peasants' holdings.

From 1861 onwards the commune was responsible to the state for the collection of taxes and redemption-charge payments. It had become, as Lenin pointed out, 'not a voluntary, but an official association'. It was useful to the state in administrative as well as in fiscal matters: the commune looked after its own affairs, under the supervision of the bureaucracy, and was held responsible for any misdemeanours committed by its members. For this reason the bureaucracy wished to preserve and bolster up the commune, to make it succeed to many of the government functions which before 1861 had fallen to the landlord. Until 1907 withdrawal from the commune was made as difficult as possible.

But the intrusion of capitalist relationships and psychology into the villages steadily undermined the *mir*. It had ceased to work in the direction of equalization, since it was coming to be dominated by the rich peasants, who increased their holdings in the periodical repartitions of land and shifted the burden of taxes and dues on to the poor. 'We want an association to fight the rich,' Lenin told 'the rural poor' in 1903. 'So the *mir* is no good to us at all.' At the same time the survival of the commune checked the enterprise and initiative of the kulaks, since it prevented the emergence of enclosed farms in which capital could profitably be invested, and restricted the concentration of land by way of mortgage and sale. The survival of the *mir* artificially preserved the economically unfit and retarded the mobility of labour.

To summarize Lenin's conclusions, then: Capitalism was already developing in the Russian countryside, and with it the stratification of the peasantry. A small minority of the richer peasants, kulaks, were prospering and were in a position to exploit their less fortunate neighbours. A much larger proportion of the peasantry was becoming so poor that they had to work as wage labourers for landlords or kulaks. In between was a considerable body of 'middle peasants', farming their own estates in a small way. This group was steadily diminishing, a small number working their way up into the kulak class, many more being thrust down into the poor peasantry.

In social terms, Lenin believed, this meant that in the revolution which was impending all groups of the peasantry would not only be ready to follow the middle-class lead, but would be far more radical than the bourgeoisie itself. 'At the present time,' he wrote in 1905, 'the peasantry is interested not so much in the absolute preservation of private property as in the confiscation of the landed estates. ... While this does not cause the peasantry to become socialist or cease to be petty-bourgeois, it is capable of becoming a whole-hearted and most radical adherent of the democratic revolution. ... Only a completely victorious revolution can give the peasantry *everything* in the sphere of agrarian reforms – everything that the peasants desire,

of which they dream, and of which they truly stand in need.'
Lenin therefore advocated a 'revolutionary-democratic dictatorship of the proletariat and the peasantry', and was prepared to envisage the Social-Democratic party entering a
provisional revolutionary government in order to maintain and
defend the revolution. Even in 1905, when he was thinking in
terms of a bourgeois revolution in the first instance, Lenin
added: 'From the democratic revolution we shall at once, and
just in accordance with the measure of our strength, the
strength of the class-conscious and organized proletariat, begin
to pass to the socialist revolution. ... We stand for unin-
terrupted revolution. We shall not stop halfway.'

Lenin's analysis led him to believe that once feudal exploitation and privilege had been eradicated, the kulaks would
share the bourgeoisie's horror of any threat of socialist revolution. And because of their dominant economic position the
kulaks might be able to sway the rest of the peasantry. But so
far as their class *interests* went, there was no reason, Lenin
argued, why the poor peasantry ((the majority in the countryside) or even the middle peasantry should actively support a
perpetuation of bourgeois rule, from which they had nothing to
gain and everything to lose. It was the development of capitalism in the villages which was causing the depression of the poor
and most of the middle peasantry. If, therefore, these groups
could be won over from the influence of the kulaks by the
Social-Democratic party, there was no reason why they should
not actively support a socialist revolution, especially if the
latter carried out its promise of freeing the villages from exploitation by kulaks as well as by landlords. That meant that
after feudalism had been overthrown by the united peasantry,
the next phase would be the lining up of the poor and middle
peasants against the kulaks, and a struggle in the villages parallel to that between proletariat and bourgeoisie in the towns.

Lenin's classification of the peasantry has proved most useful
for all subsequent inquiry into the subject; but it was of far
more than academic interest for him. It was the basis of the
different stages of Bolshevik policy towards the peasantry: (1)

with the whole peasantry against feudalism; (2) with the poor peasants against the bourgeoisie, neutralizing the middle peasantry: (3) winning the middle peasantry for the final struggle against the kulaks, by means of state pressure and experience of the advantages of large-scale collective farming. 'Only if we succeed in proving to the peasants in practice the advantages of social, collective, cooperative ... methods of cultivating the soil ... will the working class, which holds state power, be really able to prove the correctness of its position to the peasant and truly and enduringly win over the peasant millions.' For this reason Lenin always opposed any suggestion of compulsory collectivization, insisting that men were only convinced if they learnt by their own experience.

There is thus a logically consistent thread in Bolshevik policy, from the village soviets of 1905 and 1917, the committees of poor peasants in 1918, until that day in 1934 when the Soviet government proclaimed that the kulaks had been 'liquidated as a class'. Whether or not one sympathizes with the results of the policy, it is impossible not to be impressed by the solidity of presentation and the persistence which translated the modest *Development of Capitalism in Russia* of 1899 into Stalin's statement, made in November 1936 whilst introducing the new Soviet constitution, that 'the economy of our peasantry is based not on private property but on collective property, which has grown up on the basis of collective labour'. The agrarian policy which the Soviet government carried out after Lenin's death was outlined by Lenin himself, though we need not assume that he would have approved of the methods employed.

3

The most remarkable convert, if not of Lenin's writings, at least of the facts to which Lenin first called attention, was Stolypin. Stolypin had been appointed Prime Minister in July 1906, at the height of the revolutionary disturbances, in order to get rid of the State Duma and to re-establish 'order'. But it was not the old order that he re-established. The ruling class and the bureaucracy had been terrified by the peasant revolt, and Stolypin was allowed to adopt an entirely new tactic to cope with the agrarian situation. This tactic might almost be described as the Bolshevik policy in reverse: Stolypin aimed at cooperating with and assisting the development of the capitalist forces in the countryside. The revolution had wrung from the government the abolition of the land-redemption annuities. With them much of the *mir*'s usefulness to the bureaucracy also disappeared. By a series of decrees in the autumn of 1906 Stolypin gave heads of households absolute proprietary rights in their holdings, together with the right to contract out of the commune and to consolidate their strips. The ownership of these holdings had hitherto been vested in the commune, which represented all the villagers: so all but heads of households were in effect expropriated. Credits were made available – to the creditworthy – with which to purchase land from those who were willing to sell, whether the latter were landlords frightened by the events of 1905–6, or destitute peasants now graciously permitted to get rid of their allotments and go whithersoever they would. By 1917 half of the land left to the gentry in 1861 had passed into the hands of the peasantry, whether as lessees or purchasers. This supplanting of one class by another on the land can only be paralleled in the two generations before 1789 in France, or possibly (though we lack the figures) in the two generations before 1640 in England.

Stolypin's policy meant the end of the village commune, the triumph of self-help in the countryside: the government was trying to broaden its social basis and to win for itself the support not only of the landlord class, but also of the kulaks. 'We put our stake on the strong,' said Stolypin himself. The weakest went to the wall, or rather to the cities; whilst at the same time the destruction of the commune reduced the number of factory workers who still retained a link with the countryside in the shape of holdings to which they could return.

Stolypin's policy envisaged a government-sponsored agrarian revolution more drastic than the English enclosure movement at the end of the eighteenth century, and only less sweeping in its effects than the collectivization of the 1930s. If completed, it would have adversely affected the interests of a greater mass of the population than either of these two agrarian revolutions. After the dissolution of the first State Duma Stolypin's policy had to be put through by decree. Another Duma had to be dissolved, and the franchise drastically narrowed, before it was accepted. And even so, the new régime could only be maintained by violence and court martial. Over 11,000 persons were condemned to various penalties in 1907, 3,500 of them being hanged. 'Stolypin's necktie', the gallows was grimly called. There were villages in which every tenth man was flogged.

Lenin regarded Stolypin's policy as the worst of the possible alternative courses of development for Russia.

The bourgeois development of Russia in 1905 [he wrote] had already reached a point at which it was ready to demand the destruction of the existing superstructure – a worn-out, medieval landowning system. ... We are living in the period of this destruction, which the different classes of bourgeois Russia are trying, each in their own way, to carry through and complete: the peasants (plus the workers) by nationalization ... the landlords (plus the old, the 'Girondin' bourgeoisie)

by the Stolypin decrees. Reversing the order of these two possible paths of development, Lenin described them as 'the Prussian path and the American path'.

In the first case, feudal landlordism gradually grows over into bourgeois, Junker landlordism, which dooms the peasants to decades of most painful expropriation and servitude, whilst at the same time a small minority of rich peasants comes to the top. In the second case there is no landlordism, or else it is broken up by revolution, as a result of which the feudal estates are confiscated and divided into small farms. In this case the peasant predominates, becomes the only type of agriculturalist, and evolves into the capitalist farmer.

Lenin favoured the 'American path', as allowing freer and speedier capitalist development and eliminating those feudal elements from Russian society to which he felt Stolypin wished to cling. And as he pointed out, the majority of the peasant deputies in the first and second State Dumas voted for agrarian policies which coincided with the 'American path', rather than for 'Russian socialism'.

If the Stolypin policy had been given a few decades of peaceful development it might have changed the course of the revolution by splitting the peasantry and creating a strong vested interest in the countryside. But the war swept away ten million peasants and two million horses, hitting the small proprietor especially hard. The collapse of 1917 came before the new rural bourgeoisie had established and consolidated itself. Except in the Black Earth regions of the south a very small proportion of the peasantry had in fact left the *mir* by 1917. In the whole country not more than ten per cent of the peasant households had 'separated', though these were the richer families occupying some sixteen per cent of the communal land. But the proportion was so small that the 'separators' could be forced back in 1917, when 'the *mir* was living and active, though the state was in suspense'.

The Stolypin policy accelerated the process of dissolution that was already taking place in the commune; but at the same time it perhaps strengthened the loyalty of all but the richest peasants to that institution. Certainly the idea of the *mir* died hard. After Stolypin, something very like it reappeared as the village soviet; after the New Economic Policy something very different and yet very similar appeared in the collective farm, which combined the technical efficiency of the large-scale feudal estates with the communal ownership of the *mir*. So the dream of the old Narodnik leaders – a special form of Russian socialism – was realized, though as the result of a course of development very different from that predicted by those early revolutionaries.

4

The effectiveness of Lenin's analysis in the hands of the Bolshevik party was remarkably demonstrated on two subsequent occasions. Immediately after the October Revolution the Soviet government adopted the agrarian policy of the Socialist Revolutionaries, the heirs of the Narodniks, almost unchanged, and invited the support of the peasantry for a full implementation of that policy, which had conspicuously not been implemented during the eight long months in which S.R. leaders had held office. On this issue the party split; the left S.R.s joined the Soviet government and won the support of the mass of the peasantry; the old leaders of the right, thus isolated, gave little trouble and were soon absorbed by the White opponents of the revolution. Lenin had always argued that the official machine of the Socialist Revolutionary party was dominated by the interests and desires of the kulaks and the liberals, but that there was no clash of interests between the mass of the peasantry and the town workers. A Bolshevik soldier who as early as May 1917 organized the partition of the landlord's estate in his own village summed the situation up neatly: 'The Socialist Revolutionaries sitting on the district committees cried out against the illegality of our action, but did not renounce their share of the hay.'

The second occasion on which Lenin's analysis stood the party in good stead was during the period of civil war and intervention, when communications and exchange broke down and the cities and armies were suffering food shortage. Those peasants who had a grain surplus were hoarding it. In this emergency the Bolsheviks appealed to those among the peasantry who had least to gain by speculative hoarding and most to lose by the defeat of the revolution. They formed Committees of Poor Peasants in every village, gave them wide rights of search and confiscation, and entrusted to them the provision of food for the towns. The grain was extracted, the cities fed and the revolution was saved. Less than ten years later the cities repaid their debt by sending hundreds of thousands of tractors and harvesting machines to lighten the age-old toil of the poor and middle peasantry, now organized into collective farms; whilst the kulaks and speculators followed their leaders of the right S.R.s into oblivion.

The Development of Capitalism in Russia applied to a peasant country the theory which Marx had worked out for the working-class movement of the industrial West. Lenin's analysis and tactics thus have their significance outside Russia and for a longer period than Lenin's lifetime. They are important in eastern Europe today, where communist-sponsored agrarian reform has at last broken up the big estates, has in Marxist phrase 'completed the bourgeois revolution' by putting an end to the dominance of landlords, and so has created the social basis for an extension of democracy. The same analysis and tactics are being applied today in a different form over large areas of China. They will be increasingly important for the Middle East and India. Gone are the days when a Napoleon III or a Thiers could use the peasantry to suppress the revolutionary proletariat of the towns, when reactionary governments could use peasant parties as a weapon against socialism in backward and colonial countries. In eastern Europe today the peasant and agrarian parties upon which the British Foreign Office relied as elements of 'order' and stability have been split from top to bottom, or rather horizontally along class lines. The Manius and the Maceks of eastern Europe have disappeared as completely as the Chernovs did in 1918; the followers of the Mikolajczyks are being absorbed like the left Socialist Revolutionaries. And it is with a policy inspired and directed by Lenin's theory that the new peasant leaders have unseated their rivals. Modern European politics are very confusing to those who are not acquainted with the writings of Lenin.

5 'All Power to the Soviets!'

> 'The origin of Soviet power is not in a law previously considered and passed by Parliament, but in the direct initiative of the masses from below, everywhere.' (LENIN, *April 1917*)

I

In the years before 1905 Lenin's energies had been concentrated mainly on organizing the Bolshevik party, on clarifying its relationship to the liberals and the peasantry. He approached theoretical and organizational problems with such passion because he knew that the test of action was approaching. It came in the revolution of 1905, very shortly after the split of Bolsheviks and Mensheviks, a split which had been patched up, not healed.

In 1905 the Russo-Japanese War was proceeding from catastrophe to catastrophe on land and sea. The incompetence and corruption of the autocracy were shown up on a vast scale. All classes of society were disgusted with a régime which gave neither liberty nor efficiency. In December 1904 the first signal of revolt came in a victorious strike in Baku. There were demonstrations by students and professional groups in many cities. A general strike in St Petersburg followed. It was in connection with this strike that the decisive events of 22 January 1905, took place. Father Gapon, a curious and very Russian figure, half welfare-worker and half police-spy, led a demonstration of workers to petition the tsar for redress of grievances and for a constitution. As it approached the Winter Palace the procession was halted by machine-gun and rifle fire, after which Cossack cavalry rode into the helpless crowd. 1,000 persons are believed to have been killed, and many more wounded.

This 'Bloody Sunday' brought a great change in the psychology of the working class in St Petersburg. Whereas previously factory workers on strike had allowed themselves to be led by a priest and had looked to the tsar to protect them against extortionate employers, it was now made clear to all that behind the employers stood the tsarist state. Lenin had for years been attacking the 'Economists', those labour leaders who wished to concentrate on 'trade-union' matters, on alleviating working conditions whilst abstaining from revolutionary politics. Now no one could fail to see that in Russia progress towards elementary liberties was possible only by revolutionary means.

The lesson of 'Bloody Sunday' was learnt outside St Petersburg too. There were strikes in all the big cities. There were peasant revolts throughout the spring and summer. In June the crew of the battleship *Potemkin* mutinied and took over command of the vessel. In September the terrified government made a humiliating peace with Japan. In October there was a general strike, which called into existence the St Petersburg Soviet of Workers' Deputies. In August the tsar had promised a consultative assembly. On 30 October he issued a manifesto granting a legislative State Duma together with inviolability of the person, freedom of conscience, speech, assembly and association.

The then Prime Minister, Witte, subsequently said that there was 'a systematic attempt on the part of the government clique' to annul the October Manifesto. But it achieved its purpose: it split the revolutionaries. Lenin had already observed: 'the proletariat is fighting; the bourgeoisie is stealing towards power'. Henceforth all liberal groups were increasingly inclined to call a halt to the revolution, to accept the limited gains of the October Manifesto, and to attempt to work the promised constitution. This was true particularly of the Octobrists (so called because of their acceptance of the October Manifesto) and to a scarcely less extent of the Cadets (Constitutional Democrats). The initiative in direct revolutionary action passed more and more to the working-class parties. The St Petersburg Soviet became the focal point of working-class organization. Under the leadership of the Mensheviks and Trotsky there were two months of agitation until most of the members of the Soviet were arrested: but not before they had proclaimed freedom of the press and the eight-hour working day, had called for a tax strike and warned foreign investors that tsarist debts would be repudiated after the victory of the revolution. In Moscow there was a sterner struggle. There the Soviet had a Bolshevik majority, and on 22 December an armed rising took place which controlled the city for nine days before being brutally suppressed. Sporadic uprisings followed in other parts of the country, but that was the end of organized revolt. The period of sordid and bogus constitutionalism began.

2

All parties and groups began to take stock. 'They should not have resorted to arms,' said Plekhanov, who by this date had gone over completely into the Menshevik camp. 'On the contrary', wrote Lenin, 'they should have taken to arms more resolutely, energetically and aggressively.' But Lenin realized that 1905 had revealed a weakness in organization on the part of the revolutionary parties. '1905 ploughed the soil deeply and uprooted the prejudices of centuries; it awakened millions of workers and tens of millions of peasants to political life and political struggle.' But it had revealed that this revolutionary energy was unharnessed, that the power which it generated was dissipated, often enough, in isolated and uncoordinated conflicts and 'excesses'.

It was to the soviets that Lenin henceforth began to look as the focus of working-class action. In 1905 they had arisen in a dozen or more cities. They at once reappeared in March 1917. There was in Russia no really representative government, even local government: the State Dumas never wielded effective power. The soviets, assemblies of delegates from factories and working-class organizations, were the only spontaneous democratic institutions in the country. They were not the product of the armchair speculations of any political theorist, nor of the adjurations of party propagandists. They just grew. They grew up in the first instance among the town factory workers, but they had their roots in the age-old tradition of democratic organization and self-government at the lowest level, of which the village commune and the *artels* (guilds of small producers) were the most obvious examples.

Although the first soviets arose in the factories of St Petersburg and Moscow, the soviet principle could be extended to any genuine community, whether it was a village, a regiment or a battleship. The rough-and-ready soviet methods – election by show of hands in public meetings, with a right of recall, and indirect election to higher bodies – achieved real democracy for the illiterate workers far more effectively than the most elaborate constitution based upon the ballot box could have done: they brought politics to the masses in a way the latter could understand. 'It is unthinkable,' said a survey drawn up for the State Duma in May 1917, 'that a peasant woman should leave her home and children and go into the district town in order to realize her electoral rights. By what means, then, could the principle of direct and secret ballot be made operative in the villages, where fifty per cent of the inhabitants are illiterate or (allowing for the soldiers at the front) even as much as ninety per cent?' Even after the revolution two decades were to elapse before the progress of education made possible the introduction of the secret ballot.

The soviets thus meant a break with the exotic parliamentary creations of the Westernizing liberals, which was an additional argument in their favour in Lenin's eyes. The soviet constituencies were living units – a factory, a regiment – not the geographical areas of parliamentary democracy. The reality was the working community, not the isolated individual of liberal economics. Soviets could be used not only as platforms for protest and propaganda, but also as the organizing centres of revolution. In 1905 the St Petersburg Soviet had been a magnificent forum for revolutionary pronouncements and promise. The Moscow Soviet had organized and led an armed rising. In the future, as Lenin observed even at this stage, the soviets could function as both executive and legislative organs, and could provide the machinery through which the ordinary citizen might be initiated into the mysteries of governing the country which the Bolsheviks wanted him to take over. 'There is a great deal more revolutionary thought in this institution than in all your revolutionary phrases,' Lenin told his party in April 1917.

Finally, by the device of indirect election from local soviets to higher provincial and national bodies, a simple and flexible pyramidal machinery could be built up which was far more in accordance with the Russian representative tradition than the complicated system by which the State Duma was elected.

The old Narodnik dream of a community of self-governing peasant communes was never realizable, and the advent of capitalism into the villages was destroying the communes on which it was to have been based; but the tradition of self-organization and self-government re-appeared among the Russian proletariat, still closely linked with the villages from which it had so recently migrated, and gave life to the old dream in a new form. The Paris Commune as interpreted by Marx and the Russian village commune each contributed their share to the formation of Russian communism and to the structure of the Soviet state.

3

Lenin's theory of the state and of the role of the soviets is set out in *The State and Revolution*, written in the months immediately preceding the October Revolution. Lenin followed Marx and Engels in his definition of the state as 'a special organization of force; the organization of violence for the suppression of some class'. All states hitherto existing, Lenin held, had used this force on behalf of one or other of the possessing classes. The task of the working class in its revolution was to overthrow the bourgeois state and substitute for it a state which, on behalf of the overwhelming mass of the population, should use force against those whose rule was based on the exploitation of man by man. This meant that something more fundamental must happen than in previous revolutions. In bourgeois revolutions state power merely passed from one class to another: the *system* of exploitation of the many by the few remained. Indeed, the bourgeoisie on coming to power normally sought the support of its defeated enemy against its former allies, and came to a compromise agreement with the feudal land-owners. This was what the Russian liberals would have liked to be able to do in 1917 – if they could have managed it.

But for a proletarian revolution, Lenin argued, compromise with the tsarist state was impossible, since the latter existed in order to protect the property of the few against the many. Lenin had firmly grasped the fact that the higher ranks in any civil service are inevitably bound up with the class from which they are drawn and among which they live. 'Even if you write the most ideal laws – who will carry them out?' he asked his party on his return to Russia in April 1917; and he replied:

The same old officials – and they are tied to the bourgeoisie. Lenin concluded that if there was to be a fundamental recasting of society, it must be done by new men, even if these were less technically experienced than those whom they superseded.

The revolution must not mean that the new class rules, governs, through the *old* state machinery, but that this class *smashes* that machinery, and rules, governs, through *new* machinery.

In saying that the existing state machinery must be 'crushed, smashed to bits, wiped off the face of the earth', Lenin was thinking especially of the coercive aspects of the state – the standing army, the police, the bureaucracy. He specifically excepted 'the apparatus closely connected with the banks and syndicates, an apparatus which performs a vast amount of work of an accounting and statistical nature,' which must be 'wrested from the control of the capitalist', not broken up. Lenin foresaw a great future for nationalized banks.

We shall only have to cut the ugly capitalist excrescences off this admirable apparatus, make it still bigger, more democratic, more all-embracing. Then quantity will be transformed into quality. A single state bank on the largest scale, with branches in every rural district, in every factory – that is already nine-tenths of a *socialist* apparatus. It means book-keeping for the whole state, measuring and checking the output and distribution of goods for the whole state; it is so to speak the *framework* of a socialist society.

In the meantime the coercive machinery was to be replaced by 'a *more* democratic but still a state machinery in the shape of armed masses of workers, which becomes transformed into universal participation of the people in the militia. . . . *All* citizens are transformed into salaried employees of the state.' 'Officials and bureaucrats are either displaced by the direct rule of the people, or at any rate placed under special control; they not only become officers elected by the people, but they also become subject to recall at the initiative of the people.' 'Under socialism . . . for the first time in the history of civilized society, the *mass* of the population will rise to *independent* participation, not only in voting and elections, *but also in the everyday administration of affairs*. Under socialism, *all* will take part in the work of government in turn, and will soon become accustomed to no one governing at all.'

Such a state would have inexhaustible reserves of administrative personnel. 'After the 1905 revolution, Russia was ruled by 130,000 landlords. . . . And yet we are told that Russia cannot be governed by the 240,000 members of the Bolshevik party – governing in the interests of the poor and against the rich. . . . We can bring into action immediately a state apparatus of about ten if not twenty millions – an apparatus only *we* can create, for we are assured of the complete and devoted sympathy of the vast majority of the population.'

But the creation of such a state would evoke bitter resistance, which could only be overcome by force. The state organization which would have to be created for this purpose Lenin called, in conformity with Marx's usage, 'the dictatorship of the proletariat – i.e. the organization of the vanguard of the oppressed as the ruling class for the purpose of crushing the oppressors. . . . An immense expansion of democracy, which for the first time becomes democracy for the poor, democracy for the people, and not democracy for the rich: ... and suppression by force, i.e. exclusion from democracy, for the exploiters and oppressors of the people – this is the change which democracy undergoes during the *transition* from capitalism to communism.'

Lenin again followed Marx in considering that this transitional period would occupy 'a whole historical epoch'.

Only in communist society, when the resistance of the capitalists has been completely broken, when the capitalists have disappeared, when there are no classes, (i.e. when there are no differences between the members of society in their relation to the social means of production) ... only then will really complete democracy, democracy without any exceptions, be possible and be realized. And only then will democracy itself begin to *wither away* owing to the simple fact that, freed from capitalist slavery ... people will gradually *become accustomed* to observing the elementary rules of social life that have been known for centuries and repeated for thousands of years in all copy-book maxims; they will become accustomed to observing them without force, without compulsion, without subordination, without the *special apparatus* for compulsion which is called the state.

Thus Marx's 'withering away of the state' meant for Lenin that in a classless society disagreements can be settled by rational discussion. Even democracy, in the sense of coercion of minority by majority, will disappear. 'Socialism will shorten the working day, will raise the masses to a new life, will create conditions for the *majority* of the population that will enable *everybody*, without exception, to perform "state functions", and this will lead to the complete withering away of every state.'

The concluding words of Lenin's pamphlet were: 'It is more pleasant and profitable to go through the experience of revolution than to write about it,' for he stopped writing in order to take part in preparations for the October Revolution. *The State and Revolution* was not, in fact, published until early in 1918. Nevertheless, during the months preceding the revolution Lenin's tactics had been guided by the principles which he elaborated in this pamphlet, and these tactics were endorsed by the party.

The decisive features in Lenin's analysis, and those to which he attached the greatest importance, were his insistence (following Marx) on 'smashing' the old state apparatus, on replacing it by the 'dictatorship of the proletariat', and his new vision of the soviets as the political machinery through which this dictatorship could best be exercised. The west European Social-Democratic parties regarded themselves as Marxist, but Lenin, with reason, argued that they had slurred over the concept of the 'dictatorship of the proletariat', or at best had whittled away the forceful meaning which Marx had attached to that deliberately provocative phrase.

Lenin wished above all to ensure that no respect for formal legality, or even for a constitutionally expressed majority, should prevent the Bolshevik party from seizing a favourable opportunity for carrying out the changes which he regarded as essential. He was convinced (rightly, as was made clear in October and November) that the policy of his party represented the will of the majority of the population; and even if this had not been so he would have argued that the pressure of established institutions, the ruling-class monopoly of education and propaganda before 1917, the age-long habits of submission and obedience, weighted the scales unduly in illiterate Russia. The dictatorship was needed as a weapon against inertia, force of habit. 'The proletariat,' said Lenin in words which have their relevance for eastern Europe today, 'must first overthrow the bourgeoisie and conquer state power, and then use the power of the state – the dictatorship of the proletariat – as the instrument of its class for gaining the sympathy of the majority of the workers ... by satisfying their economic needs *in a revolutionary way at the expense of the exploiters*. ... They need *practical* experience to enable them to *compare* the leadership of the bourgeoisie with the leadership of the proletariat.'

4

By thus demanding a return to the traditions of Karl Marx and the Paris Commune, to a rigorously class attitude to politics, Lenin was working for a decisive breach with the theory of liberal parliamentarism and with the practice of Western Social-Democracy. This also meant a break with the Socialist Revolutionary and Menshevik parties. From March to November these parties justified Lenin's analysis by the impotence which they revealed. They completely dominated the soviets in the two capitals and the army, and indeed in the country as a whole; yet they first supported the Cadet (liberal) government set up in March, and subsequently joined in successive unstable coalitions with the Cadets. This coalition with the middle-class parties and failure to purge the civil service made it impossible for them to put their socialist programmes into action. They took refuge in the plea that any decisive changes in the structure of society must be referred to the Constituent Assembly; and the date of convening that body was repeatedly postponed.

The Constituent Assembly had long figured on the programme of the Bolsheviks; and before Lenin's return to Russia in April 1917 the policy of the party had differed little from that of the Mensheviks – critical support for the Provisional Government, a demand for peace but support for the war effort in the meantime, advocacy of a Constituent Assembly as the supreme arbiter of Russia's destiny. Lenin's return created a profound change. He called for immediate peace, immediate seizure of land by the peasantry, and the immediate transfer of all power to the soviets. He very soon began to hint that a Congress of Soviets might take the place of the Constituent Assembly. That is to say, Lenin put on to the agenda the transference of political power to the proletariat: the revolution was for him no longer merely a bourgeois revolution, and he no longer thought – as he had in 1905 – that the Social-Democratic party should enter a revolutionary coalition government. In March 1917 'state power passed into the hands of a new class, the bourgeoisie and the landlords who have turned bourgeois. *To that extent* the bourgeois-democratic revolution in Russia has been completed.' But the Provisional Government set up by the revolution, Lenin argued, was striving to reform the state machinery as little as possible, to preserve partisans of the old régime in key positions and to put obstacles in the way of 'the revolutionary initiatives of mass action and the seizure of power by the people from below'. The government had shown, too, that it was tied to the foreign policy and international connections of its predecessor. 'The workers should not support the new government: this government should support the workers,' Lenin had written from Switzerland.

In Petrograd and Moscow the soviets enjoyed as much respect as the organs of the Provisional Government. Soviets were even more firmly established in some at least of the provincial towns than in the capitals, and their range of activity in the provinces was frequently greater. In many places food distribution was in their hands, and they exercised partial control over production. From April onwards Lenin repeatedly drew the attention of party and public to a unique feature of the Russian Revolution: the existence of what he termed 'dual power'. 'By the side of the Provisional Government, the government of the *bourgeoisie*, there has developed another, as yet weak, embryonic, but undoubtedly real and growing government – the Soviets of Workers' and Soldiers' Deputies.' This government is 'a revolutionary dictatorship – a power based not on laws made by a centralized state power, but … on the direct initiative of the masses from below,' just as, for that matter, the Provisional Government itself was 'a dictatorship – i.e. a power based not on law nor on the previously expressed will of the people, but on seizure by force.' An instance of the exercise of state power by the soviets was the famous Order No. 1 of the Petrograd Soviet (14 March), which authorized all military units to elect committees with rights almost equal to those of the officers, and which was obeyed all over the country.

Yet this 'second government', under the leadership of the Socialist Revolutionaries and the Mensheviks, was giving the

Provisional Government the invaluable benefit of its moral support. The policy of the Bolsheviks, from April onwards, was to convince a majority of the workers organized in the soviets that they should take over all power in the state. 'We are not in favour of the seizure of power by a minority,' said Lenin, 'as long as the soviets have not assumed power we will not seize it.'

Lenin's simple call for 'peace, bread and land' and 'all power to the soviets' met with some early opposition within his own party and caused him to be denounced by political enemies as a 'German agent'. But as the Bolsheviks 'patiently explained' their points it became increasingly clear that they were in tune with popular sentiment. In May the Kronstadt Soviet (less than one third of whose members were then Bolsheviks) caused a great flutter by resolving that 'the sole power in Kronstadt is the soviet of workers' and soldiers' deputies'. By June the Bolsheviks were the largest single party in the Moscow Soviet; they had a majority in the workers' section of the Petrograd Soviet. On 16 and 17 July a series of spontaneous demonstrations by half a million workers and soldiers in Petrograd urged the Central Executive Committee of the Soviets to assume supreme power: 'Take power, you son of a bitch, when it's given to you,' an irate worker shouted to the Socialist Revolutionary leader, Chernov. The Bolsheviks were taken by surprise by the scale of these demonstrations no less than the Provisional Government, and did their best to prevent the demonstrations turning into an armed rising, since they felt that they had not yet sufficient influence outside the capital to be able to maintain themselves in power.

The leaders of the majority parties in the soviets did not accept the sole power thus thrown at them. The government forcibly suppressed and disarmed the Bolsheviks and their most active supporters in Petrograd and at the front. *Pravda* was smashed up and forbidden to resume publication, and forged documents were published alleging Bolshevik connections with the Germans. Lenin had to go into hiding. A new government was formed, which proclaimed its complete independence of the soviets, although it still contained representatives of the leading soviet parties. In Lenin's view the 'July Days' marked the end of dual power and the effective surrender of the soviet leaders. He declared that 'all hopes of a peaceful development of the Russian Revolution have definitely vanished,' and urged the abandonment of the slogan 'all power to the soviets'. In August Lenin predicted that the Bolsheviks would come to power by means of an insurrection not later than September or October. According to the old calendar he proved to be right.

For the next two months the Bolsheviks were a proscribed, underground party. But that helped the Provisional Government little enough. Economic crisis and inflation continued. The S.R.s and the Mensheviks had finally labelled themselves as the war parties by undertaking an offensive in July; and it was not a success. The Bolsheviks gained in influence accordingly. In September there was an attempt at a *coup d'état* by the commander-in-chief, General Kornilov, which was defeated, not by Kerensky and his government, but by the rank-and-file workers and soldiers in and around Petrograd, whom the Bolsheviks, through the soviets, swung into action against Kornilov. The railway workers stopped his trains, the telegraph operators stopped his messages. The Cadet leader, Milyukov, summed the situation up accurately when he said: 'For a short time the choice was free between Kornilov and Lenin. . . . Driven by a sort of instinct the masses – for it was with the masses that the decision lay – pronounced for Lenin.'

Everyone knew that the Bolsheviks had saved Petrograd from Kornilov: their prestige gained enormously. It was the first occasion on which the 'soviet' parties had collaborated, and as a consequence strong opposition wings began to appear within the Menshevik and S.R. parties which wished to break with the Cadets and work with the Bolsheviks. The Petrograd and Moscow Soviets gained new vigour and energy, and succeeded in evading Kerensky's order to disband the military detachments which they had formed against Kornilov. A member of the Industrial Disputes Commission appointed by the Petrograd Soviet wrote of this period: 'We were not regularly vested with any authority whatever, but the prestige of the Soviet of Workers' and Soldiers' Deputies was so great that all our decisions were unhesitatingly accepted, not only by the workers, but, strange to say, even by the employers.'

This was dual power again. Lenin once more began to contemplate the possibility of a peaceful transfer of power to the soviets: 'No class will dare to start an uprising against the soviets, and the landowners and capitalists, chastened by the experience of the Kornilov affair, will give up their power peacefully upon the categorical demand of the soviets.' Three weeks earlier, when the Petrograd and Moscow Soviets already had Bolshevik majorities, Lenin had offered the benevolent neutrality of the Bolsheviks to the S.R.s and the Mensheviks if they would form a government 'responsible solely and exclusively to the soviets', and would agree to the assumption of all power by the local soviets too.

But the leaders of the S.R.s and the Mensheviks ignored the offer, and the Provisional Government muddled on to its inglorious end. In October a 'Democratic Conference', summoned by the government as a counterbalance to the growing prestige of the soviets, was unable to produce stable majorities either for or against the coalition government, either for or against continuing the war. So the intended demonstration of the virtues of parliamentary democracy hardly gained its object. A 'Pre-Parliament' which assembled at the end of October was equally unable to produce a consistent majority for any policy at all. The liberal régime had played itself out. On the day before the Bolshevik Revolution Kerensky was in his usual state of resigning and being prevailed upon to retain office in the interests of the country.

Meanwhile the commissars of the Provisional Government had lost all influence with the army; in many of the provincial cities power dropped into the hands of the local soviets before the insurrection in Petrograd; above all, an effective transfer of power to the local elected assemblies had already taken place in the rural districts: the peasantry had revolted as a body against

a government which had done nothing to give them land despite the strong representation of the Socialist Revolutionary
party in the cabinet. On the day before the revolution an S.R.
leader, whilst denouncing the Bolsheviks, admitted that 'there is
a whole series of popular demands which have received no satisfaction up to now'; and he instanced the questions of peace,
land and democratization of the army.

At 11 p.m. on 6 November Lenin emerged from his suburban
hiding to take over the leadership of the insurrection. He caught
a tram going to the centre of Petrograd, and began to chat with
the conductress. She thought his questions extremely stupid.
'What sort of a worker are you,' she exclaimed, 'if you don't
know there's going to be a revolution? We're going to kick the
bosses out.'

The same information had reached higher circles. Next morning Kerensky's aide-de-camp reported by direct wire to the commander-in-chief: 'One has the feeling that the Provisional
Government is in the capital of an enemy which has just completed mobilization but has not yet begun military operations.'
He was right. During the course of that day dual power came to
an end when the Military Revolutionary Committee of the
Petrograd Soviet took over with ridiculous ease. There was resistance only from a handful of cadets and a women's battalion.
The one serious military incident occurred when the cruiser
Aurora steamed up the Neva to bombard the Winter Palace, in
which the government had taken refuge. Only three shells hit
the palace; meanwhile the trams were running, the cinemas
were crowded, Chaliapin was singing to his usual audience. At
7.25 on the evening of 7 November Reuter's correspondent
cabled: 'So far there have been only two casualties.' (In the
February Revolution there were over 1,400 killed and
wounded.)

At an early stage in the day's operations Kerensky left the
capital in a car flying the Stars and Stripes. When recognized in
the street, he saluted, in his own inimitable words, 'as always, a
little carelessly and with an easy smile'. So liberalism departed
after its eight months' sojourn in Russia: gracefully, conscious

of its responsibilities to history and the camera, protected from its own people by the flag of a foreign capitalist power.

5

In retrospect it is easy enough to see that the overthrow of the bankrupt and unpopular Provisional Government was inevitable. Lenin was so sure of it that he wrote (and published) an article entitled *Will the Bolsheviks retain State Power?* nearly a month before the revolution. Yet during this month Lenin from his hiding-place in Finland was carrying on a fierce struggle to convince the Central Committee of his own party of this fact. He finally got his own way by tendering his resignation (on 12 October) and threatening to appeal to the lower ranks of the party. Even after that date he wrote letter after letter with growing urgency to insist that immediate steps should be taken to seize power.

On 29 October a small group, headed by Trotsky, was nominated to direct the military side of the projected rising. But uncertainty within the leading ranks of the party continued. On the following day Lenin wrote with rising exasperation a *Letter to the Comrades*, in which he declared: 'By *waiting* for the Constituent Assembly we can solve neither the problem of the famine nor the problem of the surrender of Petrograd. . . . The famine will not wait. The peasant revolt did not wait. The war will not wait. . . . Will the famine agree to wait, because we Bolsheviks *proclaim* our faith in the convocation of the Constituent Assembly?' The members of the Central Committee who wished to await the long-promised Constituent Assembly were Zinoviev and Kamenev, who on 31 October published in the press their disapproval of the plan for armed uprising, and so by implication betrayed the Bolsheviks' design, to Lenin's extreme indignation. But even with a week's clear warning from such an unimpeachable source, the Provisional Government was able to make no adequate preparations for its own defence.

In pleading for haste Lenin was obsessed by two fears. The

first was that the army command would open the front and surrender Petrograd, together with the Baltic fleet, to the Germans, as a lesser evil than surrendering it to the Soviet. This was publicly advocated by no less a figure than Rodzyanko. John Reed reports that ten out of eleven people whom he met at tea at a Moscow merchant's house agreed that they preferred the Kaiser to the Bolsheviks; the secretary of the Petrograd branch of the Cadet party told him that the breakdown of the country's economic life was part of a campaign to discredit the revolution. Lenin thus had some grounds for suspecting that the class which still controlled the key positions of political and economic power might put its own interests before its patriotism.

Lenin's other fear was that the rising peasant revolt might get completely out of hand, and that when the Bolsheviks ultimately took over power, they might be faced with a situation of utter economic collapse and 'a wave of real anarchy may become stronger than we are'. This anxiety was, I believe, at the back of Lenin's mind from the day of his return to Russia, and that was one reason why the spinelessness and ineffectiveness of the Provisional Government enraged him so much: he feared that – as so often in nineteenth-century revolutions – it would play into the hands of a military dictator who would restore 'order'. Hence Lenin's own continual insistence on the necessity both for firm government and for good relations with the mass of the peasantry, and hence the eternally vigilant eye which he kept on generals with 'Bonapartist' tendencies. A sort of peasant anarchy, wholly destructive in its attitude, did, in fact, prevail in many parts of Russia during the civil war.

6

Lenin afterwards spoke of the days, immediately after the revolution, 'when we entered any town we liked, proclaimed the Soviet government, and within a few days nine-tenths of the workers came over to our side'. John Reed writes vividly of the hundreds of thousands of Russian men staring up at speakers all over the vast country, workmen, peasants, soldiers, sailors, trying hard to understand and to choose, thinking so intensely – and deciding so unanimously at the end. So was the Russian Revolution.'

The landslide of November is confirmed by many hostile sources. The head of the French Military Mission (a general who in 1940 still thought Lenin had been a German agent, as well as perhaps in the pay of the tsarist secret police!) had a number of interviews with leaders of the various anti-Bolshevik parties in March 1918, all of whom 'without exception and without previous discussion between themselves' agreed that any attempt to overthrow the Bolsheviks would be in vain. 'Ninety-nine per cent of the so-called "loyal" Russians were bourgeois,' Mr Bruce Lockhart noted. 'The majority of the population is in sympathy with the Bolsheviks,' concluded General Ironside gloomily after a year's experience in Archangel. There was no wholesale suppression of the opposition press during the six months immediately after the Bolshevik Revolution, no violence against political opponents, because there was no need for it. The death sentence was even abolished at the end of November, though Lenin thought this very unrealistic. When the first attempt was made to assassinate Lenin in January 1918, he treated the matter as a joke and insisted that his assailant should be liberated. The terror came later, and was a direct consequence of allied military intervention. (It was also a product of the inexperience of the Soviet administrative machine, which had no satisfactory records which would enable it to distinguish its friends from its concealed foes, and no means of bringing pressure to bear on the latter, who had nothing to lose but their lives.)

After the October Revolution, power had been assumed by the Second Congress of Soviets, which opened on 7 November, and in which the Bolsheviks had a clear majority. Lenin had already suggested that the Congress of Soviets might at popular demand be converted into a Constituent Assembly; that was the underlying assumption of *The State and Revolution*. But he had by no means convinced all the members of his own party on this point. Failure to convene the Constituent Assembly had been one of the main grounds for popular criticism of the Provisional Government. The Soviet government therefore did nothing to stop the meeting of the Assembly on 18th January.

But when it met it confirmed Lenin's view that the Constituent Assembly could not be grafted on to the Soviet structure as a sovereign body. The elections had taken place in November 1917, on party lists drawn up before the October Revolution and before the split in the Socialist Revolutionary party. That split had come from below, and had been opposed by the leaders of the party, those who headed the electoral list. The Constituent Assembly consequently contained a majority of the right-wing leaders of the S.R.s. This majority refused to accept fusion with the Central Executive Committee of the Congress of Soviets, which the Bolshevik and left S.R. Coalition offered; and so in effect the right Socialist Revolutionaries proposed a revival of dual power, which the Soviet government was not prepared to tolerate. The government parties left the Constituent Assembly, and it was dissolved on 20 January. 'Not a dog barked', as Oliver Cromwell said on a similar occasion.

There was an element of special pleading in the Bolshevik claim that the split in the S.R. party rendered the Constituent Assembly unrepresentative; but the complete absence of protest at its dissolution leaves no doubt that the left wing of the Socialist Revolutionaries, who had accepted office in the Soviet government, represented the feelings of the peasantry better than the right-wing leader, Chernov, who came to the Constituent Assembly direct from consultations with the generals at army headquarters in Mogilev. And though for decades the revolutionary parties had put their hopes on a Constituent Assembly, it is very doubtful whether these hopes were shared by the population as a whole. A survey drawn up in May 1917 for the State Duma declared categorically: 'The peasants have no ideas concerning the Constituent Assembly; in some villages its existence is unknown, notably to the women. ... The peasantry have formed *absolutely* no opinion of their own about the Constituent Assembly.' The situation may have changed by November; but in Russia there was no parliamentary tradition of any kind, and the illiterate peasantry was far more likely to be influenced by the deeds of the Bolsheviks than by the speeches of the supporters of the Constituent Assembly.

Six days after the dissolution of the Assembly Mr Philips Price cabled from Petrograd to the *Manchester Guardian*:

To regard the Convention [i.e. the Third Congress of Soviets, which met immediately after the dissolution of the Constituent Assembly] as representative of all Russia would be a mistake, because no assembly in these days can exist containing two social elements at war. But not to recognize it as the greatest force in Russia today would be a far greater mistake.

6 Small Nations and Great Powers

'The Russian revolution possesses a great international ally both in Europe and in Asia, but at the same time, and just because of this, it possesses not only a national, not only a Russian, but also an international enemy.' (LENIN *in 1908*)

I

All great revolutions have had international effects. The revolt of the Netherlands in the sixteenth century profoundly influenced the revolutionary movement in England. The English revolution of the seventeenth century had immediate repercussions in France and Holland. Its ideas only came to full fruition in eighteenth-century France and America. Lafayette and others brought back to Paris the democratic ideas of the war of American Independence. The effects outside France of the revolutions of 1789, 1830, 1848 and 1871 were immediate. But the Russian Revolution was the first in which the revolutionaries themselves were fully conscious that their actions were part of an international process and would have wished those actions to be judged not merely by their effects inside their own country.

This new international consciousness was the legacy of Karl Marx and the First International (1864–72). Its successor, the Second International, founded when Lenin was nineteen years of age, united those Social-Democratic parties which recognized the class struggle. This loose formula covered the Russian party whose programme envisaged the revolutionary overthrow of capitalism and the establishment of socialism by means of 'the dictatorship of the proletariat'; it also included the much greater number of parties with reformist programmes like that of the German Social-Democratic party. In these parties the class struggle was conceived in terms of a gradual, peaceful transition to socialism through parliamentary reform. 'The revolution', which Marx and Engels had envisaged as the only possible means of passing to a socialist order, had become for almost all the European Social-Democratic parties a phrase, a peroration, a pious hope: it was not taken seriously as an immediate practical possibility, and when the war of 1914–18 produced a revolutionary situation in a number of countries, the socialists there were for the most part totally unprepared to take advantage of it.

But in Russia during the whole period of Lenin's adult life the revolution was a fact, something with which socialists had to reckon and upon which it was essential for them to have clear views which would guide them in action. Consequently, although the Russian Social-Democratic party was small and illegal, and its representatives at Congresses of the Second International were normally émigrés, those representatives played a role there out of all proportion to the size of their party.

Lenin, more perhaps than any of the Russian émigrés, because of the close contact which he always maintained with Russia, never allowed himself to be impressed by the size and prestige of the Western parties. He became the leader of a wing of the International which laboured to put reality into the Marxist revolutionary phrases to which all the constituent parties paid lip service. This was linked up with Lenin's struggle to build up a new type of revolutionary party in Russia; the Mensheviks were supported by the majority of the Western Social-Democratic Parties, whilst the Bolsheviks found allies among the left wings of those parties.

In the process of active controversy against the 'reformists' of the Second International, and against their adherents among the Russian émigrés, Lenin wrote a series of works in which, with characteristic thoroughness, he undertook an analysis of world economic development since the death of Marx. In the light of this analysis he attempted a re-definition of the tasks of socialists in all countries. His criticism of the 'reformists' was

that they had changed Marxism from a live and developing
theory to a dead dogma of passive determinism: 'inevitable
historical forces' would bring socialism along one day, whatever individual socialists did about it in the meantime. Lenin
was the very reverse of a determinist: he always wanted to
know where he was at any given moment, so as to be able to
decide what the next step should be. His words in praise of
Engels apply no less to himself: 'He tried to analyse the transitional forms [of the state] with the utmost care, in order to
establish, in accordance with the concrete, historical, specific
features of each separate case, *from what and into what* the
given transitional form is evolving.'

2

Lenin's economic analysis was made in his *Imperialism*, published in 1916. The word 'imperialism' has been used so loosely
by so many writers that it is worth quoting Lenin's own
summing-up of his main conclusions:

> If it were necessary to give the briefest possible definition of im-
> perialism we should have to say that it is the monopoly stage of
> capitalism. ... [But a full definition should] embrace the following
> five essential features:
>
> (1) The concentration of production and capital, developed to
> such an advanced stage that it creates monopolies which play a
> decisive role in economic life.
> (2) The merging of bank capital with industrial capital, and the
> creation, on the basis of this 'finance capital,' of a financial oli-
> garchy.
> (3) The export of capital, as distinguished from the export of
> commodities, becomes particularly important.
> (4) The formation of international capitalist monopolies which
> share the world among themselves.
> (5) The territorial division of the whole world among the great-
> est capitalist powers is completed.

Lenin's immediate impetus towards writing *Imperialism*
came from controversies among socialists as to the attitude

which they should adopt to the war which had broken out in 1914. But it is as far from being an ephemeral work as *The Development of Capitalism in Russia*, which also had a controversial purpose. *Imperialism* was based on wide and purposeful reading over a long period of years; indeed, Lenin had arrived at and acted upon many of the main conclusions of his work long before *Imperialism* was published.

The Second International defined its attitude towards the threatening world war in a resolution adopted at the Stuttgart Conference in 1907, which was reaffirmed at the Basle Conference of 1912. If war should break out, despite the efforts of the working class in all countries to prevent it, then it was the duty of socialists 'with all their powers to utilize the economic and political crisis created by the war to arouse the people and thereby to hasten the downfall of capitalist class rule.' Yet in 1914 the majorities of the socialist parties in all the belligerent countries (except Russia and Serbia) supported the war. In Russia neither the Mensheviks nor the Bolsheviks voted war credits. But the former confined themselves to thus washing their hands of the war: the latter carried on anti-war propaganda in the State Duma and in the factories. In November 1914 five Bolshevik deputies to the Duma were arrested; in February they and other leaders of the party were tried and exiled to Siberia. Lenin proclaimed that 'to turn the present imperialist war into a civil war is the only correct proletarian slogan. ... The defeat of Russia is the lesser evil under all conditions.'

Lenin was by no means opposed to war as such: he was contemptuous of mere pacifism. War, he said with Clausewitz, is the continuation of politics. 'We must study the politics that preceded the war, the politics that led to and brought about the war. If the politics were imperialist politics, i.e. politics in the interests of finance capital, of the robbery and oppression of colonies and foreign countries, then the war that emerges from these politics is an imperialist war. If the politics were national-liberation politics, i.e. the expression of a mass movement against national oppression, then the war that emerges from these politics is a war for national liberation.' Lenin had no patience whatever with those Social-Democrats who cried for a peace with no annexations, whilst proposing to retain their 'own' colonies.

3

Here we come to a second aspect of Lenin's theory of imperialism which is of interest to us – his attitude towards national and colonial questions. The classic work of Russian Marxism on this subject is Stalin's *Marxism and the National Question*, first published in 1913. This work was written in the closest collaboration with Lenin, and although in what follows I shall normally quote from Lenin, the views expressed were in many cases first worked out by 'the wonderful Georgian', as Lenin called him. Indeed, it is impossible to separate the work of the two on this subject.

The Marxist view of national movements is an historically relative one: it holds that the establishment of an independent nation state is a necessary part of the bourgeois revolution, and so an essential pre-condition for the winning of democracy. Its economic basis is that 'in order to achieve complete victory for commodity production the bourgeoisie must capture the home market, must have politically united territories with a population speaking the same language.' As against what preceded them, the creation of such 'bourgeois' nations is an historically progressive step. 'One cannot be a Marxist,' Lenin wrote in 1915, 'without feeling the deepest respect for the great bourgeois revolutionaries who had an historic right to speak in the name of "bourgeois" fatherlands, who aroused tens of millions of people of new nations to civilized life in their struggle against feudalism.'

So long as a national movement would have the effect of freeing a people from foreign oppression, Marxists supported it: thus in the nineteenth century Marx was an advocate both of German and Italian national unity, and of the independence of Poland and Ireland. Until the present century national movements were largely confined to Europe and America; but

Lenin noted as a distinguishing characteristic of the new imperialism that 'the territorial division of the whole world among the greatest capitalist powers is complete'; and with this division came the development of movements for national independence in colonial and dependent countries. Russia is geographically both a European and an Asiatic country; and public opinion in Russia was deeply stirred by the struggle of the Balkan countries for independence, by the Young Turk movement, and by the Chinese Revolution. 'The right of nations to self-determination' was a very actual question in tsarist Russia. This was one more point on which the views of the Bolsheviks differed from those of the majorities in most of the other parties in the Second International.

In the Russian state there were many nationalities which enjoyed neither the rights nor the privileges of full citizens. Lenin had come up against this fact in his boyhood days in the Pugachov country on the middle Volga. At Simbirsk one of his father's friends was a member of the Chuvash national minority who had managed to get himself educated, and who devoted his life to bringing enlightenment to his compatriots. Lenin himself had a Chuvash friend at school whom he helped with his Russian.

In 1905 the Russian Revolution was supplemented by national movements in Poland, Finland, Latvia, Estonia and Georgia. As a consequence an Imperial Manifesto of June 1907 proclaimed the principle that 'the State Duma, created in order to strengthen the Russian state, should be Russian also in spirit. Other peoples who are included in our empire should have representatives in the State Duma to declare their needs, but they cannot and shall not be represented in such number as to enable them to decide purely Russian questions.' 'Persons not using the Russian language' were specifically excluded from the Duma. Stolypin's electoral law, which this manifesto accompanied, entirely disfranchised the peoples of central Asia, and drastically reduced the numbers of deputies from Poland and the Caucasus. A proposal, drawn up by Stolypin's not very liberal cabinet, to abolish some of the 650 laws imposing degrading disabilities on the Jews, was rejected by Nicholas II. In 1916 there was a rising of the native peoples in central Asia, which was brutally suppressed. Here, then, were ready-made allies, and here was a cause with which any genuine democrat could not but sympathize.

In western Europe, where independent national states were already well established by the twentieth century, 'the national question' did not seem one of particular urgency to the Social-Democratic leaders, who tended to differentiate sharply between the colonies and the metropolitan countries. The colonies, they thought, should ultimately be independent; but they envisaged a long stage of transition and trusteeship before 'their own' colonies were 'ripe' for independence.

Lenin, on the other hand, was arguing before a Congress of the Second International as early as 1907 that the demand for self-determination of colonial or dependent peoples was no less necessary in the interests of the working class of the metropolitan country than of the colony. He quoted Marx to the effect that 'a people which oppresses others cannot be free'; and he noted a remark of Cecil Rhodes's: 'The Empire ... is a bread and butter question. If you want to avoid civil war, you must become imperialists.' Lenin did not believe that genuine democracy could be established in Russia until the non-Russian peoples were treated as equal citizens and their territories were given the right to secede or become autonomous if the inhabitants wished. In order to hold down other peoples by force, armies of occupation were required, national hatred was generated, religious, class and national inequalities were increased; and all this strengthened the despotic power of the autocracy over the Russian people as well as over the peoples of the dependent nations. It is perhaps more than a coincidence that the Soviet delegate to the United Nations organization was using similar arguments in a discussion on trusteeship agreements in December 1946.

Really complete national equality, Lenin held, could only be attained under socialism, since so long as imperialism existed, the motive for exploiting other peoples would remain. But then

Lenin held the view that full democracy could also only be obtained after the overthrow of capitalism, whose economic exploitation made nonsense of political equality. So in each case – in working for democracy or in working for the independence of small nations – Lenin argued that these 'bourgeois-revolutionary' demands were also of the greatest importance for socialists, since in so far as they were achieved imperialism all over the world would be correspondingly sapped and weakened.

Lenin was careful, however, to make it clear that in supporting the *right* of nations to self-determination, and to secession if they wished it, he by no means assumed that socialists would always advocate the exercise of this right, any more than those who recognize a right to divorce wish all marriages to be dissolved. On the contrary, Lenin stressed the economic advantages of large political units, and believed that with the abolition of compulsion and with the establishment of real freedom of choice, ever larger federations of socialist states would come into existence. But the attitude of socialist parties towards secession should be determined, Lenin thought, by the interests of socialism and of historical progress in general: there was no absolute validity in national aspirations as such, but only in so far as they contributed to the struggle for democracy against more reactionary régimes. Thus in the 1850s Marx and Engels had shown no sympathy for Czech and Yugoslav national movements, because they regarded them as outposts of reactionary Russia.

4

Lenin believed that the half-heartedness of the leaders of the west European Social-Democratic parties in their support for liberation movements in the colonies, their failure to carry out their pledges to use the outbreak of war as an opportunity to work for a socialist revolution, their readiness to compromise with the ruling class, were all different aspects of the same phenomenon. 'The epoch of imperialism', he wrote, 'is an epoch in which the world is divided among the "great" privileged nations which appress all the others. Crumbs of the loot obtained as the result of these privileges and this oppression undoubtedly fall to the share of certain strata of the petty bourgeoisie, and of the working-class aristocracy and bureaucracy.' Well-paid trade-union leaders and party organizers, an insignificant minority of the working class, have acquired middle-class standards of living and a middle-class outlook, and thus have entered into what is in effect 'an alliance with their national bourgeoisie against the oppressed masses of all nations'. This alliance gives the 'opportunist' leaders their strength and influence over the working class, since behind the leaders stands not only the force of tradition and inertia but also the whole power of the ruling class, its propaganda and educational machine, and – in time of need and especially of war – prison and the firing squad.

This made Lenin regard the behaviour of the Social-Democratic leaders in 1914 as particularly despicable. Instead of mobilizing the whole party as a body to oppose the war, in which case the risk to each individual member, even to the leaders, would have been slight, the leaders of German Social-Democracy had faced each member of their party with the alternative, 'Either join the army, as your leaders advise, or be shot.'

And this, Lenin held, was the culmination of the political tendency of a whole epoch, in which the leadership of all the west European Social-Democratic parties had watered down and explained away Marxism and had acquiesced in the perpetuation of the capitalist system so long as a share of its profits went to benefit the more skilled and fortunate members of the working class. It was one more demonstration of the axiom that a people which oppresses others cannot itself be free. True Marxism, in Lenin's sense, predominated in the working-class movements only of those powers which had no old-established colonial Empire. A particularly clear example of 'labour aristocracy' was to be found in Stalin's Georgia, where the Great Russian workers enjoyed a privileged position in contrast to the native proletariat. Georgia was a stronghold of Menshevism and foreign intervention after 1917.

5

'Opportunism' in the Social-Democratic movement, then, Lenin regarded as the greatest betrayal. This determined his attitude on his return to Russia in 1917. He had on many occasions previously asked himself what a Social-Democratic government which seized power in Russia during war should do if the belligerent countries refused to accept its offer of a general peace; and he had unhesitatingly concluded that in these circumstances such a government should wage a revolutionary war. But the overthrow of the tsar in February 1917, and the advent to power of a government composed mainly of Cadets, Lenin regarded as so far only a *bourgeois* revolution: it merely brought Russia into line with the other governments which were waging war, and did not in any way affect the nature of the war or Russia's economic dependence on the Western capitalist powers. Until Russia was extricated from the war and her foreign debts repudiated, Lenin wanted the Bolsheviks to refuse support to the Provisional Government. This was in effect to advocate 'carrying over' the bourgeois revolution into a proletarian revolution, a position much more radical than that hitherto adopted by the party. For about a fortnight there was furious campaigning and counter-campaigning; then Lenin and his supporters won over the party to their view.

Lenin recognized that this policy would bring no immediate popularity to the Bolsheviks in those days of revolutionary honeymoon: it meant going against the stream for a period, during which Plekhanov said that Lenin was mad and many others said he was a German agent. But Lenin was confident that his standpoint corresponded to the real interests of the Russian masses, that it could be explained to them, and that they would soon come to see through the fine phrases of the new government. In fact, the rank and file, through the soviets, were already calling for a peace without annexations. 'When the masses declare they want no conquests, I believe them. When Guchkov and Lvov [i.e. the government] say they want no conquests, they lie. When a worker says he wants to defend his country, it is the instinct of an oppressed man that speaks in him.' It is flashes of insight like that last remark which made Lenin the leader of genius he now proved himself to be. 'Patiently explain' became his watchword for the next few weeks.

The survey drawn up in May for the State Duma noted that support for the war was diminishing. 'One frequently hears phrases like: "We shall wait until the autumn and see what happens; then the time will have come for us to turn homewards." Sentiments like this', the survey concluded sadly, 'give one food for thought.' Meanwhile the Provisional Government helped the process of disillusionment by sending a message of loyalty to the Western allies whilst at the same time it refused to publish or denounce the secret treaties binding Russia to those allies and envisaging annexations by all contracting parties. The Finnish Seim (parliament), which had an obstreperous socialist majority, was dissolved: the autonomy which the Ukraine demanded was refused.

In July, in response to pleas from the West, the Provisional Government undertook a large-scale offensive. This produced catastrophic effects in the war-weary army. Mr Philips Price noted that 'the very men who would curse Lenin as a German agent would be doing the very thing that Lenin advised them to – namely put down their arms, fraternize with the Germans, discuss socialism and the expropriation of the landlords.' 'It is terrible to die when the doors have been flung wide open in Russia,' a peasant soldier wrote home from the front long before 'Bolshevik propaganda' had reached it. Lenin's slogan of 'peace and land' bit deep into the peasant army: the officer who ordered his men to fight on was hated as the landlord in uniform. The soldiers 'voted with their feet' for peace, as Lenin put it. Nearly a week before the Bolsheviks seized power Kerensky's Minister of War declared that it was impossible to continue to fight.

So the Bolsheviks had little option but to conclude peace when they came to power. The theoretical objections to 'revolutionary defencism' no longer existed; but now the practical difficulties in continuing the war were overwhelming. The army was in a state of disintegration, the peasant soldiers rushing home to join in the scramble for the landlords' estates. The Bolsheviks at once proclaimed the right of secession for the subject peoples of Russia, denounced (and subsequently published) the secret treaties, and urged all the belligerents to enter into negotiations for a general peace. The Entente replied, not to the Soviet government, but to General Dukhonin, the anti-Bolshevik commander-in-chief, who was dismissed from his post a day or two later. The reply was a refusal, coupled with threats of most serious consequences if Russia should make a separate peace. The immediate effect was that Dukhonin was lynched by the rank and file. The flow of supplies to Russia from the Western allies ceased. 'The Russian capitalists are stretching out a hand to the British and French capitalists and landlords,' said Lenin in August 1918, echoing words he had used of the Russian workers twenty-two years earlier.

6

Since it was impossible to continue fighting in these circumstances, and yet the Soviet government did not wish to make a separate peace with Germany. Trotsky was sent to Brest-Litovsk, ostensibly to enter into negotiations with the Germans, in fact by conducting these negotiations in public to appeal to the people of all the belligerent countries to overthrow their governments and make a general peace. The terms on the basis of which the Soviet government broadcast its willingness to negotiate were, in fact, sufficiently embarrassing to all the belligerents: they included a repudiation of annexations and indemnities, and a demand for the self-determination of *all* national groups. President Wilson's Fourteen Points, announced a few weeks later, covered substantially the same ground. But the Bolsheviks had not intended their terms to be workable within the framework of capitalism, and the Fourteen Points subsequently gave the framers of the Versailles settlement considerable difficulty.

But though the Bolshevik propaganda broadcast from Brest-Litovsk brought in a rich harvest a year later, it produced no immediate revolution in the West. Appeals to the British and American governments for material assistance in the event of the war with Germany being resumed went unanswered. On the contrary: a month after the Bolshevik Revolution Clémenceau was arguing in favour of a Japanese expeditionary force being sent to Siberia. In January a Japanese cruiser entered Vladivostok Bay; already the officer commanding the 25th Middlesex at Hong Kong had been ordered to hold his battalion in readiness to proceed to the same port. British forces began to land in Murmansk at the end of February. Lenin decided that Russia must conclude a separate peace. He was afraid that England and Germany might come to terms at Russia's expense. He had to face the stubborn opposition of Trotsky and many leading party figures who had been intoxicated by the ease of the internal victory, and who were prepared to stake everything on the speedy development of revolutions in western Europe.

Lenin insisted that the preservation of the Soviet republic in Russia was the first duty of the party, and that foreign policy could not be based on speculations on the world revolution. In a series of passionate speeches he attacked the romantic attitude of the 'defencists' from the end of January to the middle of March; and at last he carried his party into acquiescence in the most unpalatable measure he had ever demanded of them. 'If you are not prepared to adapt yourself, if you are not inclined to crawl on your belly in the mud, you are not a revolutionary but a windbag: I propose this not because I like it but because we have no other road, because history has not turned out to be so agreeable as to make the revolution ripen everywhere simultaneously.'

But the leaders were divided. At one period Trotsky broke off negotiations, declared for 'neither peace nor war' (just as in 1914 he had been for 'neither victory nor defeat' in the world war) and retired from Brest-Litovsk. The Germans at once advanced and captured many hundreds of square miles of new territory; but the impossibility of further resistance was made manifest, and Lenin's policy was finally adopted, at the cost of much greater territorial sacrifices than would have been necessary if Trotsky's policy of 'sticking the bayonet into the ground' had not been pursued. By the treaty of Brest-Litovsk the Soviet republic lost a quarter of the territory of the Russian Empire and a third of its population, as well as three quarters of its coal and iron. But meanwhile the Red Army was being formed. By the middle of May it contained over 400,000 volunteers. 'As a result of this robber peace,' Lenin told Bruce Lockhart, 'Germany will have to maintain larger and not fewer forces on the East. As to her being able to obtain supplies in large quantities from Russia, you may set your fears at rest. "Passive resistance" – and the expression comes from your own country – is a more potent weapon than an army that cannot fight.' He proved to be right.

'Yielding space to gain time,' Lenin called it. 'An armistice, not peace', said *Pravda* (30 March). Lenin signed the treaty, but refused to read it. 'Of course we are violating the treaty,' he proclaimed; 'we have violated it thirty or forty times' – and this was before it was ratified. 'We have justified ourselves before the Socialist International by waiting all this time,' said a soldier delegate to the Central Executive Committee of the Congress of Soviets. In October 1918 the German General Staff decided that the morale of the troops on the Eastern front had been so undermined by Bolshevik influence that it was not worth transferring them to the West; a month later Germany had been finally defeated on the Western front, her troops were in retreat from the Ukraine, and those which remained on former Russian territory were there at the express orders of the Allied Supreme Command for the purpose of fighting the Bolsheviks.

7

For in the meantime the Allied intervention in Russia, which Lenin had feared when he insisted on concluding the treaty of Brest-Litovsk, had developed. British and Japanese troops were at Vladivostok, where Americans had also been landed to keep an eye on the Japanese. There was a British force at Archangel. It is no part of the purpose of this book to retell the sordid and shameful story of the Allied intervention, which alone made possible a revival of the Russian civil war. It is a story which has been forgotten in this country and remembered in Russia, where it cost the lives of millions of persons by battle, murder, famine and disease, and caused incalculable havoc to the economic life of the country.

The last word on the subject was uttered by the American Secretary of State on 17 July 1918, in a communication addressed to the Allied Ambassadors:

> It is the clear and fixed judgement of the Government of the United States, arrived at after repeated and very searching reconsiderations of the whole situation in Russia, that military intervention there would add to the present sad confusion in Russia rather than cure it, injure her rather than help her, and that it would be of no advantage in the prosecution of our main design, to win the war against Germany. It cannot, therefore, take part in such intervention or sanction it in principle.

Despite these fine and true words, not many months had elapsed before American troops were fighting the Bolsheviks alongside British, French and Japanese forces.

One point, however, is relevant to our present purpose, namely the effect of the wars of intervention on the international impact of the Russian Revolution. Though they failed in their primary object of rooting out the revolution, they prevented that revolution from spreading to central Europe, and perhaps farther. Thus in the spring of 1919, when a Soviet régime was fighting for its existence in Hungary, the Red Army was held in the East by the danger of a junction between Allied-controlled forces of Kolchak, which had penetrated from Siberia west of the Urals, and the British troops at Archangel. When Kolchak was finally crushed, Bela Kun's government in Hungary had been overthrown and the White terror had begun. 'A breathing space of inestimable importance', as Mr Churchill put it, 'was afforded to the whole line of newly liberated countries which stood along the western border of Russia.'

If matters had gone differently in 1919, if the vastly greater industrial resources and technical skill of central Europe had been put at the disposal of a union of soviet republics, how much human suffering and effort might have been avoided – by Russia in the 1920s, by the world after the advent of Hitler. But instead another twenty-five years were to elapse before Soviet armies appeared in the Hungarian plain – twenty-five years of narrow class dictatorship in the Balkans and most of eastern Europe.

8

In the years before the First World War there was already a group in the Second International, including figures as eminent as Rosa Luxemburg, Clara Zetkin and Liebknecht, who normally worked with the Bolsheviks in criticizing the 'reformist parliamentarism' and 'acceptance of the capitalist system' of the official leadership. During the war years a left wing organized itself inside the Social-Democratic party of almost every country, in order to oppose both the war and those party leaders who collaborated with the governments of their countries in waging it. As early as October 1914 Lenin had called for the creation of a new International, and a series of conferences of left-wing groups took place on neutral territory during the war. The October Revolution gave a new impulse, a new purpose, and above all a new leadership to these groups. Here at last was the socialist revolution of their hopes; here was a concrete achievement to defend and work for, a model to be imitated.

So when at the end of the war the official Social-Democratic parties of the principal belligerents rather shamefacedly pieced together the Second International, the glory had departed from it. It was difficult after four years of national hatred to recapture the optimistic belief in an inevitable if gradual advance to socialism and the brotherhood of man; and now in the Soviet republic there was an example of direct transition to a workers' state which strongly appealed to the war-weary masses, disillusioned with fine phrases and anxious for results. In some countries, notably Germany and Hungary, the left-wing socialists (whether organized in Communist parties or not) not only supported the Bolsheviks, but tried to follow their example. Civil war ensued, in which, just as in Russia many leading Mensheviks and Socialist Revolutionaries fought for the Whites, so official Social-Democracy was found on the side of the established order in each country where a communist-led revolt took place. A division in the international working-class movement was an accomplished fact, with the Russian Communist party the natural leader of the revolutionary wing. In March 1919 the inaugural conference of the Third (Communist) International was held in Moscow.

The Third International merely gave organizational form to a trend in the working-class movement of all countries which had already existed for many years; but it was inevitable that the local Communist parties, in working for immediate socialist revolution in their own countries, should expect guidance and support from the victorious Russian Communist party; and at the same time the 'hands off Russia' movement, which canalized the widespread sympathy felt for the Soviet government in the war-weary West, also brought relief to the Bolsheviks in their struggle against intervention. 'We deprived England, France and America of their workers and peasants,' said Lenin in December 1919. 'Their troops proved incapable of fighting us.'

Because of the atmosphere of international civil war in which the Communist International came into existence, its conditions of membership were drawn up very rigidly, largely under Lenin's influence. He applied here on an international scale the principle of 'little but good' which had been so firmly enforced in building up the Bolshevik party in Russia, and insisted on a complete breach with the political and organizational principles of Social-Democracy. This may have been unavoidable in the circumstances of the time – the fusion of the young Hungarian Communist party with the Social-Democrats in 1919 failed to produce a stable entity capable of standing up to the severe test of revolution – but it produced new difficulties. For the membership of the Communist parties in the West tended to be drawn largely from those socialists who had violently opposed the parliamentarian politics of the official Social-Democratic parties and were apt to be impatient of anything but direct strike or revolutionary action.

Lenin had attacked this type of negative reaction against parliamentarism as early as 1907, and in 1920 he wrote '*Left-Wing*' *Communism, an Infantile Disorder*, to criticize its recurrence in the Third International. We thus, paradoxically, find Lenin, a citizen of what had for so long been the least democratic European country, explaining in the name of revolutionary Marxism to the leaders of the left in western Europe that they must work in existing trade unions; that they must make use of all the institutions of parliamentary democracy in order – as 'tribunes of the people' – to give a lead to the masses; above all, that they must not merely imitate the tactics which had succeeded in Russia, but must work out their own application of the principles of Bolshevism. Revolutionary Marxism had come back to western Europe.

Until the end of 1920 Lenin agreed with Trotsky about world revolution. Later he came to think of it as an ultimate objective and an incidental ally, rather than allowing speculations as to its imminence to dominate his approach to tactical questions. But he would have agreed with Trotsky's conviction, expressed immediately after the October Revolution, that 'the Russian Revolution will either cause a revolution in the west, or the capitalists of all countries will strangle our [revolution]'. Only Lenin's thought was never confined to black-and-white, exclusive categories. He knew that the alternative possibilities in the immediate future were infinite and unpredictable. That is why he kept his head better than Trotsky over Brest-Litovsk.

In 1916 Lenin had reflected that 'the development of capitalism proceeds very unevenly in the various countries. It cannot be otherwise under the commodity production system. From this it inevitably follows that socialism cannot be victorious simultaneously in *all* countries.' 'For anyone who has carefully thought over the economic pre-requisites of the socialist revolution in Europe,' said Lenin with delicately oblique reference to Trotsky, 'it could not but be clear that in Europe it will be immeasurably more difficult to start, whereas it was immeasurably easier for us to start; but it will be more difficult for us to continue the revolution than it will be over there.' He was always convinced that 'communism cannot be imposed by force'. 'All nations will reach socialism; this is inevitable. But all nations will not reach socialism in the same way.'

In general, Lenin thought of revolutions as an historical period, not as a single event. He ridiculed 'those who imagine that in one place an army will line up and say, "we are for socialism," and in another place another army will say "we are for imperialism," and that this will be the social revolution. ... Whoever expects a "pure" social revolution will never live to see it.' Each country 'will introduce a special feature in the form of democracy it adopts, in the form of proletarian dictatorship, and in the rate at which it carries out the reconstruction of the various phases of social life.' 'In a small state adjacent to a big state in which the social revolution has been accomplished, the bourgeoisie might even surrender power peacefully.'

9

Meanwhile the Soviet Union was being consolidated as a multinational state. The soundness of Lenin's belief that national independence was as national independence did was demonstrated in the years immediately following the Bolshevik Revolution. As early as 16 November 1917, the Soviet government proclaimed the right of the peoples of the Russian Empire to self-determination, including the right of secession. At once the nationalities along the periphery of the Russian state became playthings of world politics. An independent Ukrainian government was recognized by Germany for the purpose of embarrassing the Bolsheviks in the negotiations at Brest-Litovsk, and of establishing German control in the Ukraine by the forcible restoration of the old order. The same Ukrainian government was already receiving encouragement from the Entente. The Bolsheviks in their turn helped the miners of the Donetz Basin and the workers of the industrial eastern Ukraine to establish a Soviet government in Kharkov. The Ukrainian government in Kiev became increasingly a German puppet. After Germany's defeat the Allied Command in south Russia published a manifesto to the effect that 'both the Germans and ourselves have come here not as conquerors but as champions of right. Hence their objects and ours are identical' (January 1919). The independence of the Ukraine was hardly a primary objective of either party.

A secret Anglo-French Agreement of 23 December 1917, assigned the Ukraine as a zone of influence and intervention to France, North Russia, the Baltic States and the Caucasus to England. In the Baltic States 'bourgeois' governments were set up with the aid first of German, then of British arms. The Soviet government recognized the independence of Finland, even under a bourgeois government, in January 1918; German military support helped to keep it in power. In Georgia an independent Menshevik government established itself in November 1917. The Georgian Mensheviks had never shown any interest in secession until the Bolsheviks came to power. Now, however, they called in the German army to assist in the 'preservation of their national independence'. The British subsequently took over this benevolent role, and Georgia became a recruiting-ground and supply centre for Baron Wrangel's army – the last of the White armies to survive on Soviet territory.

But where there was no outside interference, it is probable that on the whole the former subject peoples disliked the Bolsheviks less than they disliked the Whites. The latter tended to put the restoration of Great Russian privileges high on their programme – shortly after the restoration of the landlords. Denikin's proclamation of 'Russia one and indivisible' at once got him into trouble in the areas of South Russia and the Ukraine which he occupied in 1918 – even with the Cossacks, hitherto regarded as a bulwark of the old order, but now jealous of their newly won autonomy. In Turkestan a soviet régime held out during the civil war even when it was cut off from Moscow by Kolchak's government in Siberia.

Immediately after the revolution the Soviet government had formed a Commissariat of Nationalities, with Stalin as the obvious People's Commissar, and an elaborate federal structure was worked out for the Russian republic, giving regional autonomy to the various national groups. Separate soviet republics were eventually established in the Ukraine, in Byelorussia and in Transcaucasia. The needs of national defence and economic reconstruction brought them together to form the Union of Soviet Socialist Republics in December 1922. At last the whole territory of the former tsarist Empire was united by a federal constitution, of which the Decembrists had dreamed a century earlier. In the constitution of the U.S.S.R., drafted in 1923 and finally ratified ten days after Lenin's death, one of the two chambers into which the highest government organ, the Central Executive Committee of Soviets, was divided was formed on the principle of equal representation for the national groups of the U.S.S.R. The Great Russians could thus always be outvoted in the legislature by those 'persons not using the Russian language' who had been excluded from the State Duma.

There is general agreement that in its policy towards the formerly subject peoples the Soviet régime has won one of its most striking successes. Tsarism was incapable of planning of any sort, and left its industries to grow up where they would – mainly on the periphery. The events of 1917–18 revealed what a crippling blow an enemy could strike at Russia's national economy: immediately after the revolution Lenin started to occupy himself with plans for the development of industries in less accessible areas. In April 1918 he asked the Academy of Sciences to begin work on a 'Plan for the reorganization of industry and the economic development of Russia'.

A new modern civilization has arisen in western Siberia and central Asia, rich regions which the old régime lamentably failed to develop economically. And with railways, factories, tractors and the radio, education in their native language has been brought to peoples who before 1917 were wholly illiterate. A cultural renaissance has been started in Soviet central Asia whose ultimate consequences, both at home and abroad, cannot be foreseen. Among the more primitive nomadic tribes the Soviet system of government has been used to develop self-administration and some idea of democracy. The vastness of the administrative and human problems involved is suggested by an official estimate made in 1921, that over twenty per cent of the inhabitants of the Soviet republic were backward peoples either at the patriarchal and tribal stage of development or in a transitional state between tribalism and feudalism.

The mere fact that modern civilization and socialism have come together to the ancient East clearly in itself has international repercussions. In a speech to the Communist International in July 1920 Lenin restated his ideas on the colonial question. 'A certain rapprochement has been brought about between the bourgeoisie of the exploiting countries and those of the colonial countries.' In consequence, he argued, 'we communists should and will support bourgeois liberation movements in the colonial countries only when these movements are really revolutionary, when the representatives of these movements do not hinder us from training and organizing the peasants and the broad masses of the exploited in a revolutionary spirit.'

He went on to make far-reaching observations whose full significance has not yet been exhausted: 'The idea of soviet organization is a simple one and can be applied not only to proletarian but also to peasant, feudal and semi-feudal relations. . . . If the revolutionary, victorious proletariat carries on systematic propaganda among them, and if the Soviet governments render them all the assistance they possibly can, it will be wrong to assume that the capitalist stage of development is inevitable for the backward nationalities.' The truth of this statement has now been demonstrated by a generation of rising material and cultural standards in Soviet central Asia and by developments in the soviet areas of China: it remains to be seen whether Lenin's dictum will be equally applicable elsewhere.

Building Socialism in
One Country

'We destroy in order to build better.' (LENIN *to Clara Zetkin*,
1920)

I

So far we have been considering Lenin as the theorist,
organizer and leader of revolt. Barely a quarter of the book
remains to discuss his seven years' work as the head of the first
socialist state in the world. During this period the foundations
were laid on which Lenin's successors, in less than two decades,
created a great power. Merely looked upon as reconstruction of
a devastated country, the work of the Soviet government was
prodigious; but it was far more than that. This was a period of
trial and error on a gigantic scale, of experimenting with hitherto untested forms of social organization.

There were no precedents, no blue-prints. Marx and Engels
had suggested the general principles for the organization of
socialist society, both in its final classless (communist) form and
during the transitional period of 'the dictatorship of the proletariat'. But Marx and Engels had tacitly assumed that the
socialist revolution would take place in a highly industrialized
state, or else virtually simultaneously over the whole of Europe.
At first Lenin and his government hoped that the Russian Revolution would be the signal for successful socialist risings in the
West. When this hope had faded, they faced the incredibly
difficult task of applying the principles of Marxism in a single
state, and that a peasant country whose small industrial sector
had been shattered by war and civil war.

This point cannot be overemphasized in any estimate of
Lenin and the Russian Revolution. We must judge the successes
and failures of the Soviet régime not by abstract absolute stand-

ards, as this of an ideal socialist state; but as part of an experiment which had unexpectedly to be made in conditions of quite exceptional difficulty, with desperately inadequate resources, material and human, in face of the avowed hostility of almost every other government in the civilized world.

Lenin and his government, then, were trying to apply to a peculiarly Russian situation principles which they held to be universal. Some of Lenin's greatest qualities were brought out by the very difficulties of the situation – his courage, his resourcefulness, his empiricism, his readiness to compromise on anything but essentials, and his remarkably constant grasp of what were essentials, in a period when almost all his foreign critics and some even of his colleagues lost their sense of proportion at one stage or another. As a symbol of this period may be taken the spring evening in 1918 when, as so often happened, the Moscow electricity system failed; and Lenin and Gorky sat together in the Kremlin discussing by candlelight the electrification of the whole country.

2

On the morning of 8 November 1917, Lenin came down from his headquarters in the Smolny Institute, the former college for young ladies from which he had been directing the overthrow of the Provisional Government, to the Petrograd Soviet, which was meeting in another part of the same building. He was not a familiar figure at the Soviet. In the months immediately preceding the revolution he had been hiding from the police; and in any case he normally preferred to leave the managing of the Soviet to his more oratorically inclined comrades. But today there was work to do, and Lenin came forward to do it.

He allowed his audience a few minutes of rapturous applause, and then, brushing the cheering aside with a downward sweep of the arm, he went straight to business: 'The workers' and peasants' revolution, the necessity of which has always been urged by the Bolsheviks, has taken place. ... This third revo-

lution must in its final outcome lead to the victory of socialism.'

Lenin announced as the programme of the Soviet government
the immediate proposal of peace to all nations; the transfer of
land to the peasants; workers' control over the production and
distribution of goods; national control of the banks. The Second
Congress of Soviets, which met that afternoon, put this programme into action. In the next few days laws were passed
abolishing all inequalities based on class, sex, nationality or religion, and nationalizing banks, railways, foreign trade and
some of the key big industries.

On the land question the Bolsheviks neatly trumped the ace
of their most formidable opponents – the Socialist Revolutionaries, the peasant party. From the very beginning of his career
Lenin had insisted on the necessity for peasant support for a
socialist revolution in Russia. As early as 1906 he had declared
that in time of revolution the peasants should immediately take
over the land, without waiting for the convocation of a Constituent Assembly. Next year he pounced upon the fact that the
demands of the peasants elected to the First and Second State
Duma were more radical than the programme of the S.R.s, and
indeed more radical than that of the Social-Democrats.

By 1917 the programme of the S.R.s had become more revolutionary: it included the abolition of private property in land
and the distribution of the large estates by elected village committees. Though this was still from the Marxist point of view
merely a 'bourgeois-democratic' programme, nevertheless its ex-
ecution would destroy the power and influence of the landlords,
would give the peasantry a vested interest in the revolution and
by the formation of land committees with wide powers would
stimulate democratic organization in the countryside.

Above all, the Bolsheviks wanted to rouse the peasantry to
direct action, to give them confidence in their own initiative. A
resolution which Lenin introduced at the All-Russian Soviet of
Peasants' Deputies in June declared that 'the peasantry must
seize all the lands immediately, in an organized manner,
through their Soviets of Peasants' Deputies, and farm them,

without however in the least prejudicing the final settlement of the land question by the Constituent Assembly, or by an All-Russian Council of Soviets, should the people decide to place state power in the hands of such a Council of Soviets.'

Leaders of the S.R.s had been in the Provisional Government ever since the February Revolution; but they had so far done nothing to meet the demands of their radical rank and file. Twelve Bills were introduced in June 1917 by Chernov, Socialist Revolutionary Minister of Agriculture, but not one of them had become law at the time of the October Revolution. Meanwhile the land programme of the S.R.s was reaffirmed at the All-Russian Soviet of Peasants' Deputies in September, and Lenin at once promised that the Bolsheviks would put this programme into effect if they came into power. The resolution of this assembly was, in fact, embodied word for word in the Soviet law of 8 November 1917, which added that the division of the land, machinery and livestock should be entrusted to the local elected Land Committees, and should begin immediately. The S.R.s had wished the measure to await the sanction of the Constituent Assembly.

The effect was devastating. The Socialist Revolutionary party was split from top to bottom, and its left wing very soon joined the Soviet government; a left S.R. became People's Commissar for Agriculture; the peasantry as a whole was henceforth bound to the Bolsheviks by the firmest of all ties – that of self-interest; and a constructive revolutionary movement from below was set going in the countryside which made it impossible for either the peasantry or the largely peasant army to be used to overthrow the Soviet government. The pre-October régime was disarmed at a single blow. The Bolsheviks, moreover, had won one of their main points by circumventing the existing state machinery and stimulating direct initiative from below.

According to one story, a Cossack committee came to see Lenin three weeks after the revolution and asked whether the Soviet government intended to confiscate and divide up the estates of the great Cossack landowners. 'That,' Lenin replied, 'is for you to do. We shall support the working Cossacks in all their actions. ... The best way to begin is to form Cossack soviets; you will be given representation in the Central Executive Committee, and then it will be your government too.'

And the Bolshevik agrarian programme, which had envisaged large-scale cultivation in collective farms? Lenin was frank about that. In introducing the law on land to the Congress of Soviets, he said 'as a democratic government we cannot ignore the decision of the rank and file of the people, even though we may disagree with it; in the fire of experience, applying the law in practice and carrying it out locally, the peasants will themselves understand where the truth lies. ... The point is that the peasants should be firmly assured that there are no more landlords in the country, that they must themselves arrange their own lives.' That was the lesson at which Lenin was continually hammering away: the people of Russia, who for so many centuries had been the passive victims of government, at the beck and call of any landlord, employer or bureaucrat, must first of all learn the self-respect and self-confidence which could come only from practical experience in 'themselves arranging their own lives'. 'The chief shortcoming of the masses', he told the chairmen of provincial soviet executive committees in July 1918, 'is their timidity and reluctance to take affairs into their own hands.'

In June 1917 Lenin had restated his 'firm conviction that unless the land is cultivated in common by agricultural workers, with the use of the best machinery and the advice of scientifically trained agriculturalists, there can be no escape from the yoke of capitalism'. But that could wait: the important thing in November 1917 was to convince the peasants that they were free men, masters in their own house. That was a profound moral and psychological revolution, beside which everything else was of secondary importance. The October Revolution in the countryside, Lenin subsequently observed, did not begin until the summer and autumn of 1918; it was not completed until the collectivization of the early 1930s.

3

The same technique was applied in the cities. On 8 November practically the whole civil service was on strike. The Bolsheviks at once called upon all workers with office experience to put themselves at the disposal of government departments, and plastered Petrograd with placards explaining the difficulties caused by the strike and appealing for support. Ordinary people were thus taken into the government's confidence; popular resentment at delays and inefficiency in government offices, instead of falling upon the Bolsheviks, fell instead upon the strikers themselves. They lost the chance of organizing discontent, and on the contrary the government's public proclamation of its difficulties brought it new helpers.

So too in the army. When the commander-in-chief, Dukhonin, refused to obey orders to open negotiations with the Germans for an armistice, he was dismissed and – with a fine gesture – replaced by a holder of the lowest commissioned rank in the army, Ensign Krylenko. At the same time Lenin issued an appeal to the army in which he explained the situation, called on the troops to arrest counter-revolutionary generals and stop the war, and concluded: 'Soldiers! The cause of peace is in your own hands!' Dukhonin was lynched by his own rank and file; armistice negotiations began; and no general was for many months able to collect a significant body of troops to march against the Soviet government. On 29 December the principle of election of officers up to and including the commander-in-chief was introduced; the soldiers' committees and soviets were declared the supreme authority within each unit. This was, of course, a purely political and temporary move; but until peace had been concluded the army had to be kept together, and during that period the officers had to be watched. In the process the watchers learnt a good deal about democracy and about administration.

Exactly similar was the effect of a law of 12 December, which abolished 'all existing legal institutions' and replaced them by elected peoples' courts functioning in public. It must have been some time before the new courts were working at all satisfactorily, and there was no doubt a difficult period of experiment; but in the meantime judicial protection for enemies of the régime was prevented, the newly elected judges learnt their job in the best way possible, and the general public took an active interest in this experiment being tried out before its eyes and under its control. In assessing the risks of leaving the administration of justice temporarily to 'revolutionary consciousness', to 'socialist conceptions of justice', we must remember that the law of the tsarist state had been in many respects so barbarous and backward that the common sense of any reasonably enlightened person was likely to produce results more in accordance with Western ideas of justice.

As a part of the general educational process a great number of laws of vast scope were passed in the early days of the existence of the Soviet government which there was little chance of putting into immediate and detailed application. An instance was the law of 26 December 1919, obliging all citizens of Soviet Russia between the ages of eight and fifty who could neither read nor write – i.e. well over half the population – to study at state literacy schools, in their native language or in Russian, as they chose. Such laws showed that the government meant business and encouraged the initiative of the local soviets in carrying them out.

Lenin discussed this point in a speech to a party congress made on 23 March 1919. 'If we had expected that life in the rural districts could be transformed by drafting hundreds of laws, we should have been absolute idiots. But if we had not indicated in laws the road that must be followed, we should have been traitors to socialism. These laws, while they could not be carried into effect fully and immediately, played an important part as propaganda. While formerly we carried on our propaganda by means of general truths, we are now carrying on our propaganda by our work. ... Laws are instructions which call for practical mass action.' Lenin once defended the passing of a law which temporarily discontinued city soviets by saying that it was a good measure for testing their fitness; no city soviet that deserved to exist would permit itself to be dissolved! In the early days, Lenin later declared, the government said in effect: 'Here is a law; this is how we should like to have the state administered. Try it!' 'We are not afraid to confess what an acquaintance with our laws will show – that we constantly have to alter them.'

A member of the Supreme Council of National Economy described the embarrassment which his colleagues felt when, in December 1917, Lenin introduced a single draft law providing for the nationalization of all banks and joint-stock companies, the repudiation of all state loans, foreign and internal, the introduction of universal labour service, of universal consumers' societies and of workers' books for the possessing classes which alone would enable them to receive rations. They asked whether this curious medley was intended as a statement of policy, or as a law intended to be introduced at one time. Lenin solemnly said that he had the latter purpose in mind, and after considerable discussion the law was adopted. Lenin's immediate purpose here was, as he expressed it at the time, 'to fight saboteurs and counter-revolution' by instituting compulsory labour service for the possessing classes and control by workers' books; but in the process of drafting the law he had also provided for wider innovations. After the immediate practical security measures had been carried out, the general principles enunciated in the law could be put into effect at greater leisure.

At about the same time two soviet bodies produced rival interpretations of a law on workers' control in industry. One of them asked Lenin to secure legal authority for their instructions, as against the gloss put out by their rivals. After listening carefully to their arguments, Lenin replied: 'If you are really anxious to have your attitude towards workers' control put into effect, you must not rely upon authority and formal legality. You must act, you must agitate, you must use every possible method of conveying your idea to the masses. If that idea is vital and revolutionary it will force a way for itself and nullify all lifeless, even if legalized, instructions and interpretations.'

There was always this solid common sense behind Lenin's most revolutionary actions. 'Life will decide' was one of his favourite maxims; in the meantime he preferred general principles to committing himself to detailed interpretations. That could come later. The main thing was to get the new principles tried out in action.

4

The revolution, then, was the beginning, not the end: it marked a political, not an economic change. After the transfer of political power to the soviets, and after the key economic positions had been taken over by the sweeping laws passed in the early weeks of the Soviet government's existence, Lenin envisaged a slow, rather prosaic period of steady development towards socialism. Control of state power would be used to stimulate an increase in the productive forces of the backward and bankrupt country: so only a stable basis for a socialist society be laid. Lenin once analysed at length the differences between the tasks of bourgeois and proletarian revolution in general, and in particlar the difficulties which confronted a proletarian revolution in Russia:

For the bourgeois revolution, which grows up inside feudalism, new economic organizations are gradually formed in the womb of the old order, which gradually transform feudal society in all its aspects. Only one task faced the bourgeois revolution: to sweep away, to shake off and to smash all the fetters of the preceding society. By fulfilling this task every bourgeois revolution does all that is required of it; it accelerates the growth of capitalism.

The socialist revolution is in an altogether different position. The more backward the country which ... had to start the socialist revolution, the more difficult it is for it to pass from the old capitalist relations. ... The task of achieving victory over the internal enemy was an extremely easy one. The task of building up political power was extremely easy, because the masses had given us the scaffolding, the basis of this new power [the Soviets]. ... But ... exceedingly difficult tasks remained. ... The Soviet power – the proletarian power – does not inherit ready-made relationships, if we leave out of account the most developed forms of capitalism, which in fact affected only a small top stratum of industry and hardly touched agriculture at all. The organization of accounting and control in large enterprises, the transformation of the whole of the state economic mechanism into a single huge machine, into an economic organism that will so work that hundreds of millions of people can be guided by a single plan – such was the enormous organizational task that rested on our shoulders.

In May 1918 Lenin contrasted the position of the Russian Revolution with a hypothetical socialist revolution in England in the 1870s, a period at which Marx had thought a peaceful victory for socialism might have been possible if the workers 'bought off' the bourgeoisie. 'Well and what about Soviet Russia?' asked Lenin.

After the seizure of power by the proletariat, *after* the crushing of the armed resistance and sabotage of the exploiters – is it not clear that some of the same sort of conditions prevail as might have developed in England half a century ago if a peaceful transition to socialism had begun then? . . .

In Soviet Russia . . . *instead* of the absolute preponderance of workers, of proletarians, in the population, and a high degree of organization among them, the important factor making for victory was the support which the workers received from the poorest peasantry. Finally, we have neither a high cultural level nor the habit of compromise. . . . We, the proletariat of Russia, are *ahead* of England or Germany as regards our political structure, as regards the strength of the political power of the workers; but nevertheless we are *behind* the most backward West European country as regards the organization of an efficient state capitalism, as regards our cultural level and the degree of material and productive preparedness for the 'introduction' of socialism.

In Russia, therefore, the main problem as Lenin saw it early in 1918 was to raise the 'cultural level', in which he included industrial and agricultural equipment, technical skill, administrative experience and political sense, until all these reached and surpassed the west European level. And 'there is nothing communism can be built from except what has been left us by

capitalism' — 'the mass human material which has been cor-
rupted by hundreds of thousands of years of slavery, serfdom,
capitalism, small individual enterprise and the war of every
man against his neighbour for a place in the market, for a
higher price for his product of his labour.' Once, therefore, the
hope of immediate revolution in the West had been abandoned,
once the problem of building socialism in isolated and backward Russia had to be faced, Lenin foresaw a long period of
'plodding constructive work, unpretentious and unsensational.'
During this period the virtues to be demanded of communists
would no longer be fiery eloquence, dashing courage, fearless
iconoclasm, but the most sordid and despised bourgeois qualities: 'Introduce accurate and conscientious book-keeping, be
thrifty, do not be lazy, do not steal, observe the strictest discipline during work.'

5

The passages which I have just quoted were written between
March and May 1918, in the brief lull following the civil war
proper, in which the tsarist generals had easily been defeated.
But the period of economic organization and development,
which Lenin saw even then would prove so much more difficult
than the political revolution, was postponed for another three
years by the wars of foreign intervention, when England,
France, Japan and the U.S.A. financed, armed and gave military
support to puppet White generals, and all Russia became a
battlefield. At the end of 1918 the territory owing allegiance to
the Soviet government was reduced to an area roughly cor-
responding to the Muscovite state early in the sixteenth century: in three years the Bolsheviks swept over territories which
the tsars had laboriously amassed during four long centuries.

In 1921 the area under crops was less than sixty per cent and
the gross yield was less than half of the pre-war figure: the
marketable surplus had decreased to an even greater extent
with the disappearance of the big estates. In 1920 the output of
heavy industry was only thirteen per cent of pre-war, of light

industry forty-four per cent. Transport and internal trade had broken down completely; foreign trade also virtually ceased as a result of the blockade, which lasted till January 1920, and of a financial blockade, which went on until the summer of 1921. It is impossible to convey what this meant in human misery, disease and death. Nobody knows how many millions died by violence, by starvation, by epidemics. The Moscow food-cards in 1918 gave each recipient about one-seventh of the calories which the Germans received on their ration cards during the war, and about one-tenth of what was distributed in Great Britain. 'The best times then', Stalin said many years later, 'were considered to be the days on which we were able to distribute to the workers in Leningrad and Moscow one-eighth of a pound of black bread, and even that was half bran. And this continued ... for two whole years.'

So we must realize that the violent zigzags in Soviet policy in the years immediately after 1917 were caused by temporary desperate necessities: we must not allow them to confuse our estimate of Lenin's purpose, or of the lines of development and historical significance of the Russian Revolution as a whole.

In all European countries the 1914–18 war necessitated a certain amount of state regulation and control. In the Russia of 1918–20, a country already reduced to economic collapse by tsarism and military defeat in the world war, state control was a categorical necessity. The Bolsheviks had, in fact, to control much more much earlier than they had bargained for. When we recollect that even before 1917 the Russian bureaucracy was notorious for its cumbersomeness, its rigidity and inefficiency; that after 1917 a very large number of the higher civil servants had either deserted their posts, or remained only to spy and sabotage; that their places had for the most part to be filled either by the promotion of their presumably less competent subordinates or by the introduction of enthusiastic communist intellectuals or of factory workers with little or no administrative experience – when we take all this into account, it appears quite miraculous that the machine functioned at all, and we are better able to appreciate the sometimes crude methods which had perforce to be adopted in this period of 'war communism'.

To stop sabotage in industry, nationalization proceeded apace. A law of 28 June 1918, nationalized over 2,000 large-scale enterprises, and in December 1920 all factories employing more than ten workers were nationalized. These factories were managed as best they could be, partly by elected workers, partly by nominees of the trade unions, partly by such technicians as remained at work. To stop the hoarding of food in the villages the government ordered that all grain over and above that required for seed and household consumption was to be delivered to the state at fixed prices (13 May 1918). This was followed by the organization of 'committees of poor peasants' (i.e. of those who did not employ hired labour), which confiscated grain surpluses and acted as distribution agencies for food and agricultural implements in the villages. When their efforts to supply grain proved insufficient, town workers were sent into the country districts to seize grain for themselves and distribute industrial goods among those peasants who helped to collect the grain. Rationing was reintroduced in the towns, though its main effect was to distribute scarcity tolerably equitably. Money altogether lost its value.

Some Bolshevik theorists made a virtue of the necessities of war communism, praising the equality in misery as a direct transition to a communist society, and even defending the catastrophic inflation as a means of expropriating the middle classes and of escaping from the thraldom of a money economy. Lenin never committed himself to that folly. Speaking in October 1921, he admitted that 'partly as a result of the military problems that overwhelmed us and of what seemed to be the desperate position the republic was in ... we made the mistake of deciding to proceed directly to communist production and distribution. ... A very brief experience convinced us of the error of this .., which contradicted what we had previously written about the transition from capitalism to socialism, namely that it would be impossible to approach even the lower stage of communism without an intervening period of socialist accounting and control. ... We suffered a very severe defeat on the economic front.' But Lenin hardly did himself justice in associating himself with the error. In December 1919, at the height of war communism, and speaking to an audience of pioneers of collective agriculture, he declared flatly and dampingly: 'We know that we cannot establish a socialist system now: God grant that it may be established in our children's time, or perhaps in our grandchildren's time.'

6

How did the Bolsheviks manage to retain power during the intervention period, when so many states, each more powerful than Russia, were trying to overthrow the Soviet régime? In the first place, there was the fact that the international appeal of the Bolsheviks won sympathy among the populations of the interventionist states, and prevented their governments concentrating their full military power against Soviet Russia. But what were the internal factors making for the survival of the Soviet régime?

First and foremost was the support of the organized workers, which the Bolsheviks won in 1917, and never lost. But four out of every five inhabitants of Russia were peasants; and in order to obtain food to keep the war machine going at all during these years the government had to adopt pretty rough measures with the peasantry. How was it that the Bolsheviks nevertheless managed to retain peasant support?

Lenin dealt with this point in December 1919, when he asked why Admiral Kolchak, supported by the all-powerful Entente, had not been able to maintain himself in Siberia, the least proletarian area of Russia, the area which in 1917 cast the fewest votes for the Bolsheviks and the most for the Socialist Revolutionaries, whose leaders supported Kolchak; an area, moreover, where large landlordism had never been known, so that the Bolsheviks had little to offer. 'What did Kolchak lack in order to gain a victory over us? He lacked what all imperialists lack: he remained an exploiter; ... (he talked) of democracy and freedom, whereas all that was possible was one of two dictatorships: either the dictatorship of the exploiters, who savagely defend their privileges ... or the dictatorship of the workers. ... We did not draw charming pictures for the peasant; we did not say that he could emerge from capitalist society without iron discipline and without the firm power of the working class ...; but we said that the dictatorship of the workers would secure him the removal of the yoke of the exploiters – and we proved to be right.'

For the peasantry a victory of the Whites meant the return of the landlords; for the non-Russian peoples it meant the restoration of Great Russian supremacy and privileges. 'Not infrequently the peasants said, "... We are for the Bolsheviks because they expelled the landlords; but we are not for the communists because they are opposed to individual farming." And for a time the counter-revolution was able to conquer in Siberia and in the Ukraine because the bourgeoisie achieved success in the struggle for influence over the peasantry. But only a very short period of time was needed to open the peasants' eyes. They quickly acquired practical experience and said, "Yes, the Bolsheviks are rather unpleasant people; we do not like them, but still they are better than the White Guards and the Constituent Assembly." '

That was a propaganda statement, made by Lenin in July 1921, when it was of the greatest importance to convince and conciliate the peasantry. But they are amply confirmed from other sources. The U.S. commander-in-chief in Siberia declared that 'At no time while I was in Siberia was there enough popular support behind Kolchak in eastern Siberia for him to have lasted one month if all allied supports had been removed. ... I am well on the side of safety when I say that the anti-Bolsheviks killed a hundred people in eastern Siberia to every one killed by the Bolsheviks.'

Nor were the régimes which had to maintain themselves by terror even efficient. 'I think most of us were secretly in sympathy with the Bolsheviks after our experiences with the corruption and cowardice of the other side,' wrote Major Phelps

Hodges, a British officer who served with Kolchak. Exactly the same story of flagrant corruption was told of Denikin's army in south Russia. By the autumn of 1919 there was a peasant rising in Siberia and wholesale desertions from Kolchak's forces, including a whole army 20,000 strong, with its equipment and supplies.

Finally, the Bolsheviks were able to appeal to the patriotism of the peasantry and of many of the old professional classes: as their power was stabilized they came to represent Russia, whilst the counter-revolutionaries relied more and more obviously on the support of foreign invaders, whose ultimate intentions with regard to the independence of Russia were more than dubious. So the Bolsheviks – defeatists and internationalists – at length profited by a wave of peasant patriotism, a determination to clear out the foreigner and preserve the independence of Russia. This was especially true in 1920–21, when the hereditary enemy, Poland, joined the foes of Soviet Russia: the upsurge of purely Russian patriotism to which this gave rise was symbolized by the fact that Brusilov, the only really successful tsarist general during the war of 1914–17, placed his services at the disposal of the Bolsheviks. He issued a proclamation urging all Russian officers to help the Red Army.

7

But support of this kind, though it enabled the Red Army to chase the Poles back to the gates of Warsaw, did not extend to a war to spread the revolution into western Europe. So long as the wars of intervention continued it had been a primary aim of the Bolsheviks to appeal to revolutionary movements against the governments opposing them; but with the return of peace these schemes lost their immediate importance and internal questions leapt to the forefront. So long as the life-and-death struggle, in which the stakes were the whole of Europe, had continued, all other considerations had been subordinated to the prosecution of the war. But by 1921 it was clear that, whilst the forces of world capitalism were not strong enough to overthrow the Russian Revolution, supported by the earthy patriotism of the Russian peasant, neither was the Soviet government, supported by the Communist Internationl, strong enough to overthrow capitalism in western Europe. The international struggle ended in stalemate, and the Soviet government was again faced with the problem of reconstruction in Russia which it had begun to tackle in the early months of 1918.

But how different was the situation now! In 1918 the country had been economically exhausted and bankrupt, but there was a spirit of optimism and self-confidence among the workers which was itself able to overcome many difficulties. In 1921 Russia was famine-stricken, ravaged from end to end, with economic life at a standstill. The town workers, on whom the Soviet government principally relied for support, had been decimated by disease and starvation, demoralized by unemployment, and in many cases had drifted back to the villages from which they had so recently come. Worst of all were the casualties in the Bolshevik party. During the civil war party membership had normally carried with it the obligation to military service: 280,000 communists, over one-third of the entire party, including women, were serving in the Red Army in 1920. 'Communists in front' had been the slogan in every tight corner; and the Whites had shot communists, commissars and officers wholesale whenever they captured them. As a result, many thousands of experienced workers and intellectuals, potential leaders of economic and political reconstruction, were lacking when the Soviet régime most needed their services. So in 1921, not only were the tasks of the Bolsheviks infinitely more difficult than those which faced them in 1918, but the forces to whom the government could turn for support were infinitely less experienced and reliable.

Bolshevik policy was permanently affected by this shortage of skilled personnel. When in 1917 and the first half of 1918 Lenin had insisted on smashing the old state machinery and had appealed to 'the masses' to take over administrative duties, he had always tacitly assumed that there would be a guiding nucleus of seasoned and skilled political leaders. But this nucleus had been sadly reduced. For the purpose of fighting intervention, officers from the old army, doggedly supervised by political commissars, had been employed by the Red Army. Similarly many of the old civil servants had to be re-employed. Both these categories remained to form the centre of that 'soviet bureaucracy' which Lenin never tired of denouncing, but which has proved so tenacious of life.

As world revolution receded into the background, so the administrative problems of building socialism in peasant Russia loomed larger, and the bureaucracy became more and more important. This problem occupied Lenin increasingly in the last years of his life. He described the Soviet state as 'a workers' state with bureaucratic distortions', and made the removal of these distortions a main object of government policy. 'The more resolutely we now have to stand for a ruthlessly firm government, . . . the more varied must be the methods of control from below in order . . . repeatedly and tirelessly to weed out bureaucracy.' Lenin wished to see the whole population participating in the work of government: only so could the technique of administration be learned by all, and the mumbo-jumbo of a class of mandarins be avoided. 'Our aim is to ensure that *every* worker, after finishing his eight hours "lesson" in productive labour, shall perform state duties gratis.'

That is why Lenin disagreed so sharply with Trotsky over the relationship between the Soviet government and the trade unions. Trotsky wanted to transform the unions into a part of the state apparatus, to be directed from above; Lenin saw in them a democratic check on the bureaucracy, and wanted to make them 'take an active part in the work of the Soviet government by directly working in all government bodies, by organizing mass control over the activities of such bodies.' The trade unions must form a 'transmission belt' between the party and other workers. They must be 'educational organizations – organizations that enlist, that train; they are schools – schools of administration, schools of management, schools of communism.' Their function was to form 'a reservoir of state power'.

8

Lenin always insisted that the New Economic Policy introduced in 1921 was really the old economic policy of 1918, but he never attempted to disguise the fact that it was a large-scale retreat, another breathing-space, a Brest-Litovsk on the economic front. The Russian working class was depleted and exhausted. It was the largely peasant armies that had saved the Soviet republic. Industry could be restarted only if food was made available for the towns. And that meant establishing satisfactory economic and political relations with the majority of the peasantry. The key figure in the New Economic Policy was the peasant.

In March 1921 a mutiny among the garrison troops in the old Bolshevik stronghold of Kronstadt gave the danger signal, although now the troops there were no longer the proletarian stalwarts of 1917, but young peasants. But the revolt was all the more significant for that. Coming as it did when the Red Army had been checked in Poland, when hopes of a revolution in the West were fading, it led Lenin at once to advocate a drastic revision of policy.

One effect of subdividing the big landlords' estates had been to increase the number of 'middle peasants' as against both kulaks and poor peasants. The Soviet government must, therefore, Lenin argued, come to terms with the middle peasants if grain supplies were to be ensured and increased. The military methods of grain requisitioning prevalent during the civil war and the support of poor against middle peasants would no longer do: collectivization on a large scale was not practical politics until tractors and agricultural machinery could be mass produced. Therefore, as a first step, the middle peasants must be encouraged to produce food for the market and fuel for industry.

For this, fine words and promises were not enough. 'Classes cannot be deceived,' Lenin declared; 'classes are not satisfied with scraps of paper, but with material things.' And he went on to advocate freedom of trade for the small producer, and the production of consumers' goods in the towns to be exchanged against agricultural products. Above all, the peasant was to be secured against arbitrary requisitioning and forced sales, and thus encouraged to develop his farm. After he had paid the graduated tax in kind the peasant must be free to sell the remainder of his produce where and to whom he pleased. In 1922 Soviet law was codified so as to define the position and rights of private enterprise within the socialist state. Lenin, against the opposition of the majority on the Central Executive Committee, obtained the appointment of a public attorney to 'safeguard revolutionary legality' and enforce some degree of judicial uniformity.

Lenin defined the basic principles of the N.E.P. as (1) All land and 'the commanding heights in the sphere of production' to be owned by the state; (2) free trade for small producers; (3) state capitalism – the attraction of private capital, concessions to foreign capitalists, and the setting up of mixed companies of private concessionaries and state nominees. These principles were not adopted without a struggle among the Bolsheviks themselves.

The Kronstadt mutiny, in fact, came at a time of acute controversy inside the party. Trotsky and his supporters wished to continue and indeed intensify the measures adopted under war communism, and were advocating universal regimentation and militarization of labour as a way out of the economic crisis. This policy was opposed by the trade-union leaders, and, as Lenin at once pointed out, it ignored the peasantry altogether – i.e. the rank and file of the army. An historian of the Red Army has suggested that the Kronstadt mutiny 'sounded the death knell of Trotsky's ambitions to become the head of the Communist party and the ruler of Russia.' Such a view exaggerates, I think, the importance of Trotsky in the party, and it ignores the fact that the New Economic Policy had been adopted before the mutiny. But Kronstadt certainly helped to make N.E.P. acceptable to the party.

But the proclamation of the policy was only half the battle. Lenin henceforward devoted his energies to goading on his followers with jibes to deliver the goods to the peasantry. The

N.E.P., he declared, was a real test of the fitness of communists to govern the country. 'The capitalist is operating by your side. He is operating like a robber, he makes a profit, but he is skilful. But you – you are trying to do it in a new way: you do not make any profit; your communist principles, your ideals are excellent, they are written out so beautifully that you deserve to be living saints in heaven – but can you do business?' Lenin put this question to a party congress in March 1922, and he answered on behalf of the peasants: 'You are fine fellows, you defended our native land, that is why we obeyed you; but if you cannot do business, get out!'

With his usual frankness Lenin summarized the political philosophy underlying the N.E.P. to a Congress of the Communist International in July 1921. 'We had to show the peasantry that we could and would quickly change our policy in order immediately to alleviate their want ... We are the state power. To a certain extent we are able to distribute the burden of privation, impose it upon various classes, and in this way relatively alleviate the conditions of certain strata of the population. ... We must distribute the burdens in such a way as to preserve the power of the proletariat. This is the only principle by which we are guided. ... The peasantry in Russia has certainly gained more from the revolution than the working class. ... We are assisting the peasantry because it is absolutely necessary to do so in order that we may retain political power.' At the same time cooperative trade would provide a school of administration for the peasantry similar to that which Lenin expected the trade unions to provide for the town workers.

9

We are now in a position to appraise the N.E.P. as Lenin saw it. The October Revolution had put power into the hands of the Soviet government. The revolution had been completely successful in its negative aspect: tsar and landlords had gone for ever. But it had not led to the immediate introduction of social-

ism, and could not do so in a country so economically backward as Russia. Many communists had hoped that the more
advanced workers of the West would come to the help of the
small Russian proletariat. But by March 1921 it was clear that
there would be no immediate revolution in western Europe and
that the peasantry – the mass of the population, which had
rallied to the support of the government against foreign intervention – would not stand any prolongation of the measures
which the war had necessitated. 'To a certain degree,' Lenin
observed, 'our revolution was a bourgeois revolution.' So far the
peasantry had benefited most by the expulsion of the big landlords and the division of the land. But the Bolsheviks had done
more than 'carry the bourgeois revolution to its logical con-
clusion'; they had also established the soviet government and
the soviet system throughout the Russian state, and thus 'facili-
tated the struggle for the socialist revolution.' What more was
required?

Lenin's answer to this question throws a flood of light on
Soviet policy for the next two decades. 'It is possible to carry
out the socialist revolution in a country in which the small
farmer producers constitute the overwhelming majority of
population only by means of a number of special transitional
measures which would be totally unnecessary in countries with
developed capitalism.' State power, in fact, had first to be maintained (and that necessitated good relations with the peasantry)
and then used to develop the productive resources of backward
Russia until the economic level of western Europe had been
reached. 'Communism', as Lenin summed it up in a famous epi-
gram, 'equals Soviet power plus the electrification of the whole
country.' From 1921 onwards the interests of socialism were
held to demand every possible measure which could stimulate
productivity, provided only these measures did not threaten the
one essential – the maintenance of the soviet system, of political
power in the hands of the Communist party.

With this single reservation, the Soviet government was prepared to go to almost any lengths to get the economic life of

Russia going again. Private trade was restored; the rouble was stabilized; some small factories which had been nationalized were handed over to producers' cooperatives, and one or two were even restored to private ownership; negotiations for concessions were started with foreign capitalists; and every effort was made to restore confidence in the stability of the Soviet régime. 'The Russian is a bad worker compared with workers of the advanced countries,' Lenin had stated unflatteringly but truthfully in 1918; and although he also noted the historical reasons for this backwardness, he nevertheless proceeded to suggest a series of drastic remedies, along lines which were to become familiar in the later history of the U.S.S.R.: the personal responsibility of officials and business executives must be insisted on, lest they hide behind anonymous corporate bodies; piece-work rates and the Taylor system must be experimented with, competition must be encouraged. Piece-work rates were, in fact, adopted in 1918; but these and similar measures – preferential rations, bonuses – appealing to personal, selfish interests came into full effect only with the N.E.P.

The egalitarians were shocked; they felt that the age of revolutionary heroism was being left behind too rapidly; but Lenin was firm in his common-sense approach, for which, in any case, he could find ample support in the writings of Marx and Engels. 'Self-interest will develop production,' Lenin wrote for *Pravda* of 31 October 1921; 'and we must first develop production at all costs. ... Not directly relying on enthusiasm, but aided by the enthusiasm born of the great revolution, and on the basis of self-interest, personal benefit and business principles, you must set to work in this small-peasant country to build solid little bridges leading to socialism by way of state capitalism.' Bourgeois experts, however hostile to the Soviet state, must be utilized: 'the idea that we can build communism by the hands of pure communists, without the assistance of bourgeois experts, is childish. ... Socialism cannot be built unless advantage is taken of the heritage of capitalist culture. ... The bourgeois experts must be so encompassed by organized, creative and harmonious work that they will be compelled to fall in line with the proletariat, no matter how much they resist and fight at every step.' 'No price for tuition will be too high if only we learn intelligently.'

10

Unsympathetic foreign economists, who had seen nothing but chaos in the desperately heroic days of war communism, now saw nothing but surrender to capitalism in the N.E.P. But Lenin kept his head, and knew perfectly well what he was up to, what the limits of manoeuvre were. When Krassin, head of the Russian Trade Delegation in England on one occasion suggested that the state monopoly of foreign trade might be modified in the interests of commercial negotiations with England, Lenin declared that he had gone mad. Without the state monopoly 'any rich industrial country can completely break down a tariff barrier. To do so it need only introduce an export bounty on the goods exported to Russia on which we levy a duty. Any industrial country has more than enough money to finance such a bounty, and thus any industrial country can inevitably break down our home industries' – a point which advocates of 'the open door' in undeveloped countries always choose to overlook.

'It is We or They, the capitalists or the Soviet government,' said Lenin in a famous slogan which summarized his view of the N.E.P. And whilst some Soviet economists began to dream of a permanent N.E.P., of the kulaks 'growing into socialism', Lenin was already thinking in terms of the next phase of the electrification of the whole country, of the planned development of heavy industry, of the collectivization of agriculture, of preparations for the world war which he already saw was inevitable.

As early as February 1918 a Soviet law had spoken of 'the development of collective farming ... with a view to the transition to socialist agricultural economy,' and nine months later Lenin was discussing 'the method of transition to a communal and cooperative form of land-cultivation.' He again stressed the role of the state in creating not only the technical possibility of collective agriculture, but also the readiness of the peasantry to take advantage of the possibility. Answering Kautsky's jibe that 'small peasants have never passed to collective production under the influence of theoretical convictions', Lenin asked, 'But what, dear Kautsky, if the peasants *lack implements* for small production, and the proletarian state *helps* them to obtain agricultural machinery for the collective cultivation of the soil – is that a "theoretical conviction"?' 'All forms of individual agriculture are ... to be regarded as transitory and having outlived their time,' said a resolution passed by the Central Executive Committee of the Congress of Soviets in February 1919. Some state and collective farms had already been set up on confiscated big estates. By 1920 there were over 16,000 of them, and they received steady government encouragement.

Lenin returned to this point in one of his last writings, the famous article *On Co-operation*, which he dictated painfully, twenty minutes at a time, in January 1923. Before the revolution, he said, Marxists had scorned utopian dreams of a direct transition to socialism by means of the cooperative movement. But now all had been changed by the transfer of political power. 'Indeed, since state power is in the hands of the working class, since this state power owns all the means of production, the only task that really remains for us to perform is to organize the population in cooperative societies.'

Formerly the Bolsheviks had emphasized revolution, the conquest of political power, and had sneered at the 'reformists'; henceforth – now that power was conquered – peaceful, organizational, educational work, 'reformist methods', were what counted. The political revolution had made possible 'gradualism' in economic development. Many members of the Communist party had some difficulty in making the psychological readjustment necessary to grasp and act upon this fact, and Lenin never tired of bringing it to their attention. The substitution of the N.E.P. for war communism he likened to the adoption of siege warfare after a failure to take a citadel by storm. 'Heroism displayed in prolonged and stubborn organizational work on a national scale is immeasurably more difficult than, but at the same time immeasurably superior to, heroism displayed in an insurrection.'

The Russian Communist party, as Lenin well knew, was walking along a very tightly stretched rope over an abyss. The party was trying to lead the population on lines of which it had a clear conception, and yet 'among the people we are as a drop in the ocean, and we shall be able to administer only when we properly express what the people realize.' In order to carry out its programme the lead had to be retained in its own hands, and yet the forces of the party had been tragically depleted during the wars of intervention. In order to build socialism it was first necessary for the Communist party to raise Russia to the economic and cultural level of Western capitalism, in the first instance in a certain sense to rebuild capitalism; to use the motive of self-interest to construct the prerequisites of a classless society, to use state control to encourage individual initiative, dictatorship to educate the population up to democracy. This vast process of re-educating a population of 150 millions put an almost intolerable strain on the vitality and disinterestedness of the educators themselves. The party members needed Lenin's sharp eye on them all the time, his sharp tongue goading, jeering, deflating, attacking complacency as the unforgivable sin. 'Our worst internal enemy is the Communist who occupies a responsible (or for that matter not very responsible) Soviet post and enjoys universal respect as a conscientious man.'

II

But that was only half the story. Woolly and unbusinesslike comrades, of whom there were many, Lenin bruised with brutal wit. He delighted in deflating the eloquence of those who were party members and nothing more. But he had no use for defeatists. To civil-service jokes about Russia under the N.E.P. being 'a man on crutches', Lenin retorted fiercely, 'Russia was battered for seven years, and thank God we *can* get about on crutches.' And for all his insistence on the necessity of appealing to the most sordid motives to start the economic life of the country up again, for all his sneers at those who neglected the humdrum tasks of the day for scholastic squabbles or dreams of utopias, Lenin was swift to seize upon and eloquent to encourage any development in which he thought he detected a germ of a new spirit. The source of his will-power was in the last resort his deep belief in the goodness of man, of man un-trammelled by property.

In the summer of 1919 a movement grew up spontaneously among the local organs of the Communist party whereby Satur-day, a non-working day, was devoted to voluntary unpaid labour about the urgent tasks of the war. The movement spread, until in May 1920 15,000 party members and 25,000 non-party workers participated in these *subbotniks* in Moscow alone. The cynic would have seen in this development merely a means of extracting so many more man-hours from the exhausted workers of Russia. But Lenin looked far deeper than that. 'If we were to ask what the present economic structure in Soviet Russia is,' he wrote,

we should have to say that the foundations of socialism are being laid in large-scale production, that the old capitalist econ-omic system is being remoulded. . . . What we obtained from the expropriation of the landlords and capitalists was only the pos-sibility of building up the initial forms of socialism; but there is nothing communistic in that yet. . . . If there is anything communis-tic in our present system in Russia it is the subbotniks, and only the subbotniks. . . . Something has been created . . . in the form of unpaid labour organized far and wide to meet the needs of the state as a whole, something absolutely new, which runs counter to all the old capitalist rules, something superior to the socialist society which is triumphing over capitalism.

It is characteristic of Lenin that after this paean in praise of the new spirit of man which he saw emerging from the squalor and suffering of the civil war – it is characteristic that he should add that he could not yet be sure of the degree of success won by the subbotniks, as he had not received full and precise stat-istics; but, he concluded, in any case subbotniks should be a useful touchstone for detecting the lazy and unserious party member. 'The dreamer in the Kremlin,' as Mr H. G. Wells called him, could be almost sordidly practical.

12

In December 1922 Lenin had a second brain haemorrhage. Paralysis of the right hand and leg set in. From this time onwards he took very little part in practical affairs. He died in January 1924, at the age of fifty-three. He was still in the prime of life, but had worn himself out. Only one British Prime Minister in the last hundred years (Lord Rosebery) reached the highest office before he was fifty-two, the age at which Lenin was forced into virtual retirement.

Lenin died before the victory of the new social order was assured in the U.S.S.R.; but he knew that

what has been won by the Russian Revolution is inalienable. No power on earth can deprive us of that. ... For hundreds of years states have been built on the bourgeois model, and now for the first time a non-bourgeois form of state has been discovered. Maybe our apparatus is pretty bad, but they say that the first steam engine invented was bad too: they are not even sure whether it worked or not. ... But the point is that now we have got steam engines. However bad our state apparatus is – still it has been created: a most important historical invention has been made, a proletarian type of state has been created. Therefore let the whole of Europe, let thousands of bourgeois newspapers, carry news about the horrors and poverty and sufferings which the workers endure in our country – still all over the world all workers are attracted to the Soviet state.

Part Three
After the Revolution

8 Lenin and the Russian Revolution

'Everyone acts according to his lights.' (LENIN *in August 1918, after being shot by Fanny Kaplan*)

I

Lenin died on 21 January 1924. Kalinin, the peasant who, as he put it, had climbed with dirty feet into the place of the tsars, wept when he announced the news to the Congress of Soviets. For a week Lenin lay in state, whilst long queues waited for hours in the bitter cold to see him. 'The Bolsheviks can organize much,' wrote Mr Duranty to the *New York Times* on 27 January, 'but it is not their propaganda which draws these hundreds of thousands to Lenin's feet.' From the construction of the mausoleum in the Red Square in which Lenin lies embalmed until its closure during the Nazi-Soviet War there was every day a long procession of simple people who wished to pay their respects to the dead leader. Lenin's body, like those of the saints of the Orthodox Church, has not known corruption. Trotsky was among those who opposed the suggestion that the corpse should be thus preserved, and it is doubtful whether such a process would have a similar effect in the more sophisticated West of today. But in seventeenth-century England Oliver Cromwell's effigy lay in state for many weeks after his death, 'multitudes daily crowding to see this glorious but mournful sight'. There can be no doubt that the decision to embalm and exhibit Lenin's corpse responded to a real popular sentiment. His dead body has been seen by millions more than ever saw him alive.

Every civilization has to make of its great men what it can, to assimilate their ideas into its own idiom. In Tadjik and Kazakh legend Lenin was as high as the hills, as the clouds; in Dungan folk-lore he was brighter than the sun and knew no night. The Oyruts say that he had a sunbeam in his right hand, a moonbeam in his left; the ground trembled under him. For the Uzbeks Lenin was a giant who could shake the earth and move great rocks in his search for the fortune hidden in the hills; he could solve the most puzzling riddles. In Kirgiz story he had a magic ring, with the help of which he overthrew the power of the evil one and liberated the poor from wrong and injustice. He is reputed to have arrived in Armenia on a white horse, to lead the people. In another legend Lenin was a Titan struggling against Asmodeus, the friend of the rich and privileged, the worst enemy of the poor. Asmodeus strove to kill Lenin, but the light from the hero's eyes put him to flight. Lenin then seated himself upon an eagle and flew to Dagestan, where he stirred up war against the rich, and finally flew back to the cold regions to write books of truth for the people. For the northern Ostyaks Lenin was a great seal hunter who slew the rich fur-traders and gave the booty to the poor; similarly, the Nentsy think of Lenin as the most expert of all sailors, who overcame his enemies in combat, seized their dogs and reindeer, and divided them among the poor. Sholokhov's Cossacks visualized Lenin as a Don Cossack.

In pre-revolutionary Russia the church, as in the Catholic West in the Middle Ages, realized that its abstract ideas must be made concrete by means of images, icons, banners, relics and other objects which could be grasped by the senses of the matter-of-fact and uneducated peasantry. (The iconoclasm of the puritans and others was due to the fierce intellectual arrogance of those who have just become acquainted with abstract ideas and with their power over material objects.) The Bolsheviks have exposed the mystification with which the church attempted to give a miraculous power to its images and relics, and so to itself; but they use some of the same technique of conveying ideas, because they are speaking to the same people. It is thus necessary on the one hand to recognize the historical background to the Bolshevik propaganda idiom, which otherwise might seem naïve and unsophisticated, and on the other to realize that although techniques of the Orthodox Church have been taken over, they are put to very different uses. Lenin is not worshipped; no one pretends that there is anything miraculous in the scientific processes by which his corpse is preserved: his body in the mausoleum in the Red Square and his portrait replacing that of the tsar on the walls give something concrete for the peasant mind to grasp, dominated as it is in everyday life by material objects and material objects only.

But it is Lenin's words, Lenin's ideas, which are really authoritative in the Soviet Union today. Generalissimo Stalin liked to be called Lenin's disciple. Even Trotsky, who before he joined the Bolshevik party in August 1917 had been one of Lenin's keenest critics in the Social-Democratic movement, after 1924 found it expedient to claim Lenin's authority for his views. I have, I hope, succeeded in the preceding pages in giving some general impression of what Lenin stood for. But it may be worth summarizing now the personal characteristics in him which in a peculiar way symbolized the Russian Revolution, and for which he is especially remembered today.

2

First and foremost Lenin symbolizes the Russian Revolution as a movement of the poor and oppressed of the earth who have successfully risen against the great and the powerful. That was and is the most important single fact about the revolution, both in its internal and international effects. 'It's a fine thing, the revolution,' said a peasant whose holding had increased from eight to eighty-five acres. 'Everyone is in favour of it. They don't like the Communist party, but they like the revolution.' That was the authentic note of the underdog, which scarcely any first-hand observer of the revolution failed to capture. An old worker who drove John Reed back to Petrograd from Tsarskoye Selo a few days after the October Revolution, 'swept the far-gleaming capital with an exultant gesture. "Mine," he cried, his face all alight. "All mine now! My Petrograd." '

All who met him agree that Lenin, for all his aristocratic

origins and his middle-class upbringing, was very close to the common average Russian. In his campaign against those who in March 1918 wanted to fight a revolutionary war against the Germans, the severest thing Lenin could find to say was that they 'look at things from the point of view of the knight, who said as he died, sword in hand, in a beautiful pose: "Peace is disgraceful, war is honourable!" They argue from the point of view of the aristocrat: I argue from the point of view of the peasant.' 'There was in him something of kinship with the soil of Russia,' said his political opponent, Axelrod; 'the most earthly of all who have walked this earth of men,' said the poet Mayakovsky. Lenin summed up the period in 1889 when his mother tried to get him to manage the family estates by saying: 'My relations with the peasants became abnormal.' When he lived in the Kremlin Lenin quite unaffectedly continued to live in the most simple style, sleeping on an iron bedstead in a carpetless room; he did not even consciously dispense with luxuries, but was merely rather irritated when anyone tried to force them upon him. Presents of food which peasants sent in to him during the famine he invariably gave away.

In its feeling for the ordinary man Lenin's thought was fundamentally democratic. Many people before him had expressed the view that genuine democracy was impossible without socialism; but Lenin insisted on the converse, that socialism without democracy was impossible, since '(1) the proletariat cannot achieve the socialist revolution unless it is prepared for this task by the struggle for democracy; (2) victorious socialism cannot retain its victory and lead humanity to the stage when the stage withers away unless it establishes complete democracy.' Lenin praised the soviets because they represented 'democracy for the poor, for the people, not for the rich', and thought of the main function of trade unions in a socialist state as the education of the workers in democratic habits.

Lenin summed up his conception of what the revolution meant by reporting a conversation that he had overheard in a railway train. An old woman had said with surprise: 'Today you don't need to be afraid of a man with a gun. When I was in the forest a man with a gun met me, but instead of taking away my firewood he helped me to gather some more.' Lenin used this remark to illustrate the change in the basis of the state, the fact that its power was now used to protect the masses of the population. Under tsarism it had been used against them.

He returned to the same point in a later speech, though here he is thinking more of the liberating effect of the revolution on things of the mind: 'Hitherto the whole creative genius of the human intellect has laboured only to give the advantages of technique and civilization to the few, and to deprive the rest of the most elementary necessities – education and free development. But now all the marvels of technique, all the conquests of civilization, are the property of the whole people, and henceforth human intellect and genius will never be twisted into a means of oppression, a means of exploitation. We know this: surely it is worth striving with all our might to fulfill this stupendous historic task? The workers will carry out this titanic historic labour, for there are vast revolutionary powers slumbering in them, vast powers of renovation and regeneration.'

Lenin's style of speaking seems to have had the same characteristics of straightforwardness and simplicity as his arguments. He was not a great orator, in the sense in which Kerensky and Trotsky were. All observers agree that he dominated his audiences by sheer force of intellect and personality: 'I came out into the street feeling as if I had been beaten over the head with a flail,' said a political opponent. Lenin dispensed with gesticulation, oratorical tricks and flourishes, flattery of his audience or appeals to their emotions. 'His words always brought to my mind the cold glitter of steel shavings,' wrote Gorky; Clara Zetkin said he threw out sentences 'like unhewn blocks of granite.' 'What a professor lost to the world!' said the great historian Kovalevsky. All his speeches got down at once to hard thinking, and as soon as he had made his points he stopped, often abruptly. In his maturer years his self-confidence was supreme, because based on a deep analysis of the facts, and he spoke with a breathless urgency and conviction which swept all before it. Morally, the oratorical spell-binder Trotsky 'was as incapable of

standing against Lenin as a flea would be against an elephant,'
observed Bruce Lockhart.

3

Lenin possessed a second quality which symbolizes the achievements of the revolution as a whole. It is the quality which on
Maurice Baring's first visit to Russia most impressed him as typical of the ordinary Russian – humaneness. The attempt to overthrow the Bolsheviks after the revolution produced cruelties
indeed; but the revolutionary process abolished a régime of despair and created a new world of hope. 'Children, these hands
cannot write,' said an old peasant in 1918, holding up his worn
and calloused hands to a group of schoolchildren; 'they cannot
write because the only thing the tsar wanted them for was to
plough. But you, children of a new Russia, you can learn to
write. Oh that I might begin again as a child in the new
Russia!'

These were the new things which affected popular judge-
ment. Murder and sudden death, alas, had been familiar enough
for centuries in Russian history. Gorky, who on many occasions
in the hard times of civil war intervened with Lenin on behalf
of suspected intellectuals, and never met with a refusal, says of
him: 'I have never met anyone in Russia, the country where the
inevitability of suffering is preached as the general road to sal-
vation, nor do I know of anyone who hated, loathed and despised all unhappiness, grief and suffering as Lenin did.' Lenin
once said to Gorky, after enjoying a Beethoven sonata: 'But I
can't listen to music too often. It affects your nerves, makes you
want to say stupid, nice things, and stroke the heads of people
who could create such beauty while living in this vile hell. And
now you mustn't stroke anyone's head – you might get your
hand bitten off. You have to hit them on the head, without any
mercy, although our ideal is not to use force against anyone.
H'm, h'm, our duty is infernally hard.'

He told the sculptress Claire Sheridan that her allegorical
figure of Victory was not to his taste because it was too beauti-

ful: victory was not like that. ('I'm not criticizing you,' he added mildly; 'only please don't touch me up.' Like Cromwell, he wanted to be represented warts and all.)

Hatred of tyranny and oppression because of their degrading effects on oppressors and oppressed alike was the moral force behind Lenin's loathing for tsarism, for any system of economic exploitation or national subjugation. Yet in 1916 he did not forget to remind Poles and Finns, 'who now justly hate the Great Russians for the executioner's role they are playing, that it is not wise to extend this hatred to the *socialist* workers and to a socialist Russia; that economic interests as well as the instinct and the consciousness of internationalism and democracy demand the speediest establishment of intimacy among and amalgamation of all nations in a socialist society.'

In September 1919, when Soviet Russia was still involved in desperate war, Lenin was talking to women about their 'actual position of inferiority because all the housework is thrust upon them, ... the most unproductive, most barbarous and most arduous work,' which 'is extremely petty and contains nothing that facilitates the development of women.' To Clara Zetkin Lenin spoke angrily of 'the calm acquiescence of men who see how women grow worn out in petty, monstrous household work, their strength and time dissipated and wasted, their minds growing narrow and stale, their hearts beating slowly, their wills weakened.' He advanced it as a further argument in favour of collective agriculture that 'small peasant economy means small separate households, with the women chained to them.' And he called on women themselves to take the lead in establishing the communal institutions which would help to liberate them from their burden and make them free and equal citizens.

A small enough beginning; but it is such small and concrete beginnings that are recollected, as was Lenin's speech to schoolteachers extolling the dignity of the part they had to play in the creation of a socialist society, and ending up by saying it was 'most, most, most important of all to improve their material position.' In pre-revolutionary society the position of the

teacher had been so lowly that without that postscript the rest
would have been mere verbiage. One of the few non-political
occasions on which Lenin is recorded to have lost his temper
was with a father who said it did a healthy child no harm to get
tired. Lenin, who had got off his bicycle to help the child up a
steep hill, said furiously, 'People like you should not be allowed
to have children at all.'

4

Thirdly, Lenin stands for all those qualities going to make the
Russian Revolution – purposefulness, realism, common sense,
will-power, pugnacity – which were most conspicuously lacking
in the pre-revolutionary intelligentsia satirized by Chekhov. At
the London Congress of 1903 a political opponent complained to
Lenin, 'How oppressive the atmosphere is at our Congress! This
bitter fighting, this agitation one against the other, this biting
controversy, this uncomradely behaviour!' 'What a splendid
thing our Congress is!' Lenin replied. 'A free and open struggle.
Opinions stated. Shades of disagreement made clear. Groups
have taken shape. Hands have been raised. A decision has been
taken. A stage has been passed. Forward! That's the stuff for me!
That's life! That's something different from the endless, tedious
logic-chopping of your intellectuals, which doesn't stop because
the question has been settled, but because they are too tired to
talk any more. . . .' After this Congress Lenin stood out almost
alone of the leading émigrés against all five of his old editorial
colleagues on *Iskra*, persons much older than himself, great
names in the Russian revolutionary movement. Unperturbed,
and relying on support from inside Russia, he wrote *One Step
Forward, Two Steps Back*, in which he proclaimed, 'It would be
criminal cowardice to doubt even for a moment the inevitable
and complete triumph of the principles of revolutionary Social-
Democracy, of proletarian organization and party discipline.'
What, as the Menshevik Dan asked, are you to do with a man
like that? For such self-confidence there is only one
justification: success.

Fourteen years later, in June 1917, the Menshevik leader Tseretelli, full of ministerial dignity and grandeur, proclaimed at the First Congress of Soviets that there was not a single party in Russia which would agree to take over sole power. 'Oh yes there is,' called out Lenin from the back of the hall. 'Our party is prepared at any moment to take over the entire power.' They laughed then; but Lenin knew exactly what the possibilities were. He disliked nothing more than revolutionaries who, instead of soberly calculating the realities of any given situation, resorted to 'the vigorous waving of small red flags'. 'To wage a socialist revolutionary war without railways would be the most sinister treachery,' he told the romantic supporters of Trotsky during the Brest-Litovsk negotiations. 'I am absolutely horrified,' he had written to the party leaders in Russia in 1905, 'that people can go on talking about bombs for more than six months without making a single one.' 'Insurrection is an art,' Lenin proclaimed on every appropriate occasion, an art which he studied with his usual thoroughness. The tactics of October – the seizure of the telephone exchange and General Post Office, of bridges, railway stations and the power station, and above all the maintenance of a vigorous offensive – were based on the conclusions which Lenin had arrived at after studying the revolution of 1905 and the military textbooks of the Geneva libraries.

I have already given many instances of Lenin's assiduous attention to detail. He corrected all the proofs of *Iskra* himself, to make sure there were no mistakes. In 1917, as soon as he heard about the February Revolution, Lenin wrote to Madame Kollontai in Sweden to give her his views on the tactics henceforth to be adopted; he did not fail to note that domestic servants could now be interested in politics. In the hectic days immediately after the October Revolution Lenin found time to see a totally unknown armless man who came to see him with proposals for a producers' cooperative; and remembered to ask the person to whom he passed him on what action had been taken. When Gorky asked Lenin how he found time to bother about improving the food service in the Kremlin canteen, he replied in tones of amazement: 'About rational feeding?' as though the obvious importance of the question when so expressed was conclusive. During the civil war an unknown civilian who joined a group of military experts examining an anti-aircraft artillery gadget impressed all the soldiers by his technical knowledge: they were even more impressed when they discovered that the civilian was Lenin. Not long before his active political work ceased altogether, in January 1922, Lenin was writing to the editor of a newspaper published for poor peasants, asking how many letters were received from peasants and what subjects they dealt with; and that such reports should be sent to him every two months.

With all Lenin's attention to theory, he on occasion showed a cheerful empiricism in action. He once quoted Napoleon's '*On s'engage, et puis on voit*'; he might equally well have quoted the remark attributed to Cromwell: 'No one ever rises so high as he who knows not whither he is going.' 'As though one can set about a great revolution and know beforehand how it is to be completed,' Lenin said on another occasion. On 27 November 1917, he paraphrased Cromwell's famous 'Trust in God and keep your powder dry' in reply to a left Socialist Revolutionary orator who had said that the work of the Constituent Assembly would depend on the mood of the country. 'But I say, "Trust in the mood, but don't forget your rifles." '

Cromwell and Napoleon are the men of action with whom it is most natural to compare Lenin, though his period of real power was briefer than theirs. But Lenin was what Cromwell and Napoleon were not – also a thinker. No one since Calvin has so combined the two roles. Lenin was profoundly conscious of his debt to the past, both the Russian past and the past of west European civilization as interpreted by Marx. He spoke severely to enthusiastic young communists who had as little use for 'bourgeois culture' as they had for the barbarous tsarist educational methods: 'We must understand that in place of the old system of teaching, the old cramming, the old parade-ground discipline, we must substitute an ability to take possession of the whole sum of human knowledge, in such a way that communism is for you not something learnt by heart, but something that you have thought out for yourselves, conclusions which seem irresistible in the light of modern education.'

Yet at the same time Lenin was tolerant of the intolerance of the young, and of the sometimes wild experiments which flourished in the first years of liberation from the tsarist censorship and ecclesiastical orthodoxy. He used words which help us to understand much that has happened since his day in the world of Soviet art and letters. 'The chaotic ferment, the feverish search for new solutions and new watch-words, the "Hosanna" for certain artistic and spiritual tendencies today, the "crucify them" tomorrow! – all that is unavoidable.'

Lenin's own preference in literature was for the classical masters: he did not admire the experimental declamatory poetry of Mayakovsky, for instance, though he respected him for his influence on the younger generation. But he had no use for literary cliques. 'It is not important what art gives to a few hundreds or even thousands of a population as great as ours. Art belongs to the people. It must have its deepest roots in the broad mass of the workers. ... So that art may come to the people, and the people to art, we must first of all raise the general level of education and culture.' The neglect of education under the old régime, and the impossibility of remedying this during the civil war, had been 'a cruel crime against the happiness of the rising generation'.

Lenin's own thought, at least as revealed in his published writings, was always strictly functional. Not even Marx ever wasted less time on irrelevant speculation. There are no excursuses in Lenin's works; no lingering by the way; no relaxation: and his most original work is usually cast in polemic form, so that it is not always easy reading today. Lenin's wider reflection comes through in occasional flashes, when suddenly a vision of the future seems to him of immediate practical use. When talking about foreign trade under the N.E.P., Lenin unexpectedly said, 'Where we conquer on a world scale, I think we shall use gold for building public lavatories in the streets of several of the largest cities in the world'; but now it was needed to buy imports. Four years before the revolution Lenin leapt upon the idea of underground gasification of coal; successful experiments for thus ending the back-breaking toil of the miner have been carried out since the establishment of Soviet power. Socialism for Lenin was above all a more rational organization of society, in which human energy should not be dissipated, human effort not frustrated and misapplied. Only a socialist order could bring full human liberty to more than a minority of the population.

On the rare occasions when Lenin discussed 'the higher phase of communist society', he did so with almost exaggerated caution. This stage, he considered, would only be reached when 'the antithesis between mental and physical labour, ... one of the principal sources of modern *social* inequality,' had disappeared. But when or how this would happen he refused to discuss, 'since no material is available to enable us to answer such questions.' 'It has never entered the head of any socialist to "promise" that the highest phase of communism will arrive.' In *foreseeing* its arrival the great socialists 'presupposed both a productivity of labour unlike the present and a human being unlike the present man in the street'. But when that stage has been reached, ' "the narrow horizon of bourgeois rights", which compels one to calculate, with the shrewdness of a Shylock, whether he has not worked half an hour more than another – whether he is not getting less pay than another – this narrow horizon will then be left behind. There will then be no need for society to make an exact calculation of the quantity of products to be distributed to each of its members; each will take freely "according to his needs".'

5

Finally, there is Lenin the Russian patriot. We are coming to appreciate the patriotic aspect of the Russian Revolution more nowadays, but it is one of which Soviet citizens have always been conscious. The revolution freed Russia from foreign domination and exploitation, gave her an independent foreign policy, defeated the foreign invader, and through manifold sufferings created the powerful U.S.S.R. of today. As early as 1931 Prince Mirsky found that patriotic acceptance of Soviet policy brought the émigrés to a closer study of the Russian Revolution and its leader, and led him to conclude that it was impossible to accept the October Revolution without accepting Lenin's ideas. The Russian Revolution was Lenin's revolution.

For all his years of exile and his internationalism, Lenin was no cosmopolitan. He had a very special affection for and pride in Russian literature, especially Chernishevsky and Tolstoy. Lenin's own Russian prose is a model of efficiency and straight-forwardness. His writings contain no fireworks about patri-otism, because there were too many of them on the other side of the barricades. But he was ready on occasion to 'crawl on his belly in the mud' if the interests of Russia and the revolution required it, as when he went in person to the German Embassy to apologize for the assassination of Count Mirbach, whom a Socialist Revolutionary had killed in the hope of embroiling the Soviet government with Germany.

Above all Lenin is identified with the economic and political reconstruction of the U.S.S.R., with the building of socialism. His wife said after his death: 'Let not your deep, abounding grief be expressed in outward honours for Lenin's personality. Monuments to his name and sumptuous ceremonies – all that in his life he valued so little, found them all so tiresome. Remem-ber how much poverty and lack of order yet exist in our country. If you want to honour Lenin's name, build crèches, children's homes, schools, libraries, hospitals, sanatoria, and above all try so to act that by you his will be done.'

I have tried to suggest how in dealing with all the major problems which faced the Bolsheviks Lenin stood for the appli-cation of Marxism to the specifically Russian historical situ-ation. His greatness lies in that he perfectly represented the point of intersection of the old and the new, the Russian and the Western, the peasant and the socialist. Unlike the pro-German tsarist court, the French-speaking aristocracy, the Anglophil Cadets, unlike even the Westernizing theoreticians in the revo-lutionary movement – the Mensheviks and Trotsky – Lenin knew the Russian peoples and valued their traditions. So he was able to carry the masses with him. But on the other hand, unlike the Slavophils and the Narodniks, he did not despise the achievements of Western science and thought. When a code of Soviet laws was being drafted Lenin wrote to the official concerned: 'Get hold immediately of all the literature there is and consider the experience of the west European countries. But don't stop there (that is the most important of all). Don't be satisfied with "Europe", but go further. . . . Don't miss the smallest chance of intensifying state interference in private property relations.'

It was because of his Marxism that Lenin was able to succeed where the Narodnik terrorist Zhelyabov had failed, in 'giving history a shove'. To the old fatalistic Russia, with its philosophies of passivity and suffering, the revolution brought the tremendous hope that men might control their own destinies.

With Gorky, the greatest contemporary Russian man of letters, who was also his intimate friend, Lenin often during his last illness discussed the meaning of the revolution which had been his life's work. Gorky records a remark from one of these conversations which might form Lenin's epitaph. Speaking of the rising Soviet generation, Lenin said, 'These will have much happier lives than we had. They will not experience much that we lived through. There will not be so much cruelty in their lives. . . . And yet I don't envy them. Our generation achieved something of amazing significance for history. The cruelty, which the conditions of our life made necessary, will be understood and vindicated. Everything will be understood, everything.'

9 The Significance of the Russian Revolution

'Do not copy our tactics, but think out for yourselves the reasons why they assumed these peculiar features, the conditions that gave rise to them and their results.' (LENIN *to Caucasian Communists, April 1921*)

I

The dissolution of the Communist International in May 1943 seemed to proclaim that the Russian Revolution was not for export, and to underline the national character of that revolution. Yet there can be no doubt that the influence of the U.S.S.R. and of communism is far greater today than at the time of Lenin's death: they have acquired the prestige of demonstrated success. The French Revolution, the only comparable event in history, produced no international organization, and yet its influence was world-wide and lasting. So it is likely to be with the Russian Revolution, with or without a Communist International, so long as there are problems in the world for which the experience of that revolution offers a hope of solution.

What are likely to be the long-run influences of the Russian Revolution? It is still too early to attempt any final reply to this question, and I have indicated here and there in the course of this book what some of the effects of the revolution may be. But it may be convenient to summarize.

First, soviet experience in the bringing of modern civilization to backward peoples, and especially the development of the soviet system and collective farms as means of self-government for agrarian peoples – this is bound to have enormous influence in eastern Europe, Asia, and perhaps ultimately in Africa and South America.

Secondly, the U.S.S.R. has demonstrated in practice that socialism is a system which can work even under the most unpromising conditions, and the Soviet single-party system has put before all the highly industrialized countries of the world one possible solution of the conflict between economic planning and political liberty. It is becoming increasingly obvious that absolute freedom of private enterprise is incompatible with the demand of the average citizen for freedom from want and freedom from fear. The achievement of rational planning, full employment and universal economic security in the U.S.S.R. has already set standards of which the rest of the world is having to take account. The example of soviet socialism is bound to have the most incalculable effects in all countries over a very long period of time, including those west European and North American countries where the soviet techniques of government are least likely to be adopted in their entirety.

Finally, reinforcing both these points, the Russian Revolution has demonstrated that the common people of the earth (and indeed of what was a very backward country) can take over power and run the state infinitely more effectively than their 'betters'. From this point of view each victory of the Red Army in the late war against Germany was more inflammatory than a score of manifestos issued by the Communist International.

Lenin made this point in the article, *Will the Bolsheviks be able to retain State Power?* which he wrote over three weeks before the October Revolution: 'We have not yet seen the strength of resistance of the proletarians and poor peasants. For the full measure of this strength will be revealed only when power has passed into the hands of the proletariat, when tens of millions of people who had been crushed by want and capitalist slavery will see from their own experience, will *feel* that state power has passed into the possession of the oppressed classes. ... Only then shall we be able to see what untapped forces of resistance to capitalism are latent in the people, ... who until then had been politically dormant, languishing in poverty and despair, having lost faith in themselves as human beings, in their right to live, in the possibility that they too might be served by the whole force of the modern centralized state.'

The victories of the Red Army in 1918–21 and 1941–5 realized the dream of an Englishman three hundred years ago, who said that in a communist society 'if a foreign enemy endeavour to come in, we shall all with joint consent rise up to defend our inheritance, and shall be true to one another'.* An unknown soldier from the 548th Division was overheard saying the same thing just before the October Revolution: 'When the land belongs to the peasants, and the factories to the workers, and the power to the Soviets, then we'll know we have something to fight for and we'll fight for it.'

2

I come back continually to this feature of the Russian Revolution, that it uplifted the poor and the downtrodden and improved their lot in the everyday things of life. This is what most impresses in contemporary records of the revolution, and this is what is likely to be its most widespread and lasting effect. For the everyday things of life still mean most to the poor and downtrodden, and they are still the majority of the population of the world. The best image of the revolution that I know comes in an account written by a very simple man who by a chapter of accidents found himself sent as a Soviet commissar to a rural district in the far eastern island of Sakhalin. There at a meeting an old peasant said to him, 'See here, Mr Chief, we have heard rumours here that in Russia there is now war among the Russian people, between some that are called Bolsheviks and others that are called Whites. They say that the Bolsheviks fight for the people so that there shall be no tsar any more and so that the land shall be taken from the lords and given to the peasants; we understand little of that. Will you tell us about it?' Another peasant, an exiled convict, said: 'It would have been fine if the tsar had given the land to the peasants. I remember that in my

---

* *Selections from the Works of Gerrard Winstanley* (ed. Hamilton), p. 103.

village in Russia in my time there used to be talk that land would be allotted any day, but we never got it.' The commissar, who was very far indeed from being a Bolshevik, concluded: 'There was general excitement. Everybody talked, and I could see that they thought something new had happened, from which they would live better.'

That is what the revolution meant.

Some Books
for Further Reading

V. I. LENIN. *Selected Works*, 12 vols. Lawrence & Wishart, London, 1936–8.

N. KRUPSKAYA. *Memories of Lenin*, Martin Lawrence, London, 1943.

M. GORKY. *Days with Lenin*, Martin Lawrence, London, 1933.

L. FISCHER. *The Life of Lenin*, Weidenfeld & Nicolson, London, 1965.

B. H. SUMNER. *Survey of Russian History*, Duckworth, London, 1948.

SIR J. MAYNARD. *Russia in Flux: Before October* and *The Russian Peasant and other Studies*, Collier Macmillan, London, 1962.

T. SHANIN. *The Awkward Class: Political Sociology of Peasantry in a Developing Society: Russia 1910–1925*, Oxford University Press, 1972.

R. KINDERSLEY. *The First Russian Revisionists: A Study of Legal Marxism in Russia*, Oxford University Press, 1962.

I. M. MAISKY. *Before the Storm*, Hutchinson & Co, London, 1944.

D. J. FOOTMAN. *Red Prelude*, Cresset Press, London, 1944.

SIR B. PARES. *The Fall of the Russian Monarchy*, Jonathan Cape, London, 1939.

SIR BRUCE R. LOCKHART. *Memoirs of a British Agent*, Putnam, London and New York, 1932; Penguin Books, Harmondsworth, 1950.

L. TROTSKY. *History of the Russian Revolution*, Cresset Press, London, 1957.

J. V. STALIN. *The October Revolution*, Martin Lawrence, London, 1934.

J. V. STALIN. *Leninism*, 2 vols, Allen & Unwin, London, 1928, 1933; Lawrence & Wishart, 1940.

GORKY, STALIN et al. eds. *The History of the Civil War in the U.S.S.R.*, Collet, London, 1950.

K. E. HOLME. *Two Commonwealths*, Harrap, London, 1945.

M. DOBB. *Soviet Economic Development Since 1917*, Routledge & Kegan Paul, London, 1960.

E. H. CARR. *The Bolshevik Revolution, 1917–23*, 3 vols, Penguin Books, Harmondsworth, 1969.

I. DEUTSCHER. *The Prophet Armed, Trotsky 1879–1921*, Oxford University Press, 1954.

I. DEUTSCHER. *The Prophet Unarmed, Trotsky 1921–1929*, Oxford University Press, 1959.

I. DEUTSCHER. *The Unfinished Revolution: Russia 1917–1967*, Oxford University Press, 1967.

Maps

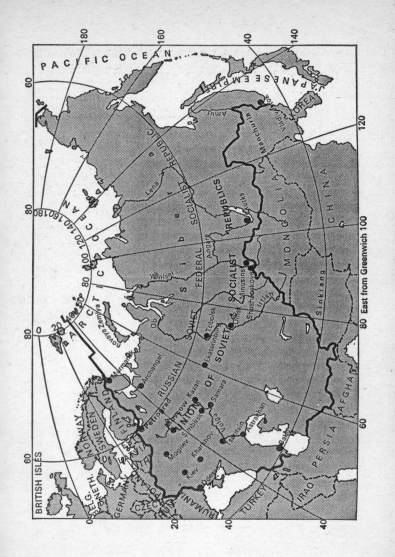

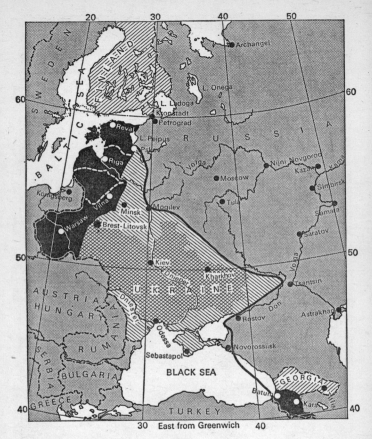

- ---- Western boundary of Russian Empire, 1914
- Territory occupied by Germany, March 1918
- Territories ceded to Germany and Turkey under the Treaty of Brest Litovsk
- Satellite states of Germany set up by the Treaty of Brest Litovsk

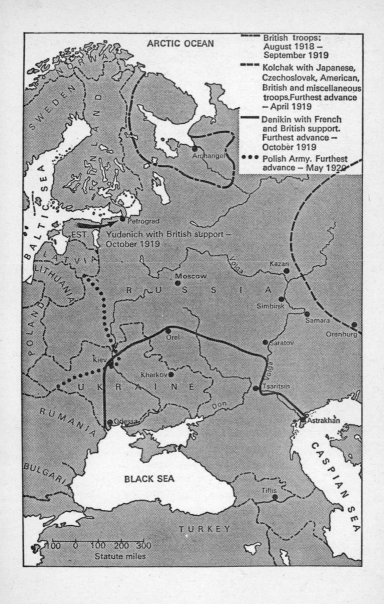

ARCTIC OCEAN

British troops:
August 1918 –
September 1919

Kolchak with Japanese,
Czechoslovak, American,
British and miscellaneous
troops. Furthest advance
– April 1919

Denikin with French
and British support.
Furthest advance –
October 1919

Polish Army. Furthest
advance – May 1920

NORWAY

SWEDEN

FINLAND

BALTIC SEA

Archangel

Petrograd

EST.

LATVIA

Yudenich with British support –
October 1919

LITHUANIA

POLAND

R U S S I A

Moscow

Volga

Kazan

Simbirsk

Samara

Orenburg

Orel

Saratov

Kiev

Kharkov

U K R A I N E

Don

Volga

Tsaritsin

RUMANIA

Odessa

Astrakhan

BULGARIA

BLACK SEA

CASPIAN SEA

Tiflis

T U R K E Y

100 0 100 200 300
Statute miles

Index

Index

More About Penguins and Pelicans

Also by Christopher Hill in Pelicans:

The World Turned Upside Down
Radical Ideas During the English Revolution

'This book will outlive our time and will stand as a notable monument tothe man, the committed radical scholar, and one of the finest historians of the present age ... It exemplifies in a striking fashion his great qualities ... easily the best work so far written on the subject' – *The Times Literary Supplement*

'Brilliant ... he depicts with marvellous erudition and sympathy the profound rationality of the Cromwellian "underground" ' – David Caute in the *New Statesman*

'Incorporates some of Dr Hill's most profound statements yet about the seventeenth-century revolution as a whole ... no one has demonstrated more cogently how literary sources can break the barriers that even now keep the poor in the background of history' – *Economist*

'Christopher Hill has that supreme gift of being able to show us the seventeenth-century world from the inside' – Arthur Marwick in *New Society*

Reformation to Industrial Revolution

Christopher Hill

The period 1530–1780 witnessed the making of modern
English society. Under the Tudors England was a society
of subsistence agriculture in which it was taken for
granted that a fully human existence was possible only
for the landed ruling class. In 1780 England was a
national market on the threshold of industrial revolution,
and the ideology of self-help had permeated into the
middle ranks. A universal belief in original sin had
been supplanted by the romanticism of 'Man is good'.
And the first British Empire had already been won and lost.

In this masterly study one of the great historians on the
seventeenth century analyses the transformation of
British society and the complex interaction of economic,
cultural and political ferment of the seventeenth
century and its influence on the revolutions in trade and
agriculture, which in their turn prepared English society
for the take-off into the modern industrial world.

'This formidable little book – its range of information is
remarkable and it is stuffed with fruitful hypotheses –
is rather a commentary than an analysis' – Peter Laslett
in the *Guardian*

'There is clearly no lack of controversial matter here:
Mr Hill has fulfilled an important function of a good
social history' – *The Times Literary Supplement*

God's Englishman

Oliver Cromwell and the English Revolution

Christopher Hill

Cromwell told the Barebones Parliament that 'indeed there
are histories that do give you narratives' but went on
to declare that what mattered was 'those things
wherein the life and power of them lay'.

This is not conventional biography, but a number of
brilliant interpretative essays, analysing the forces
which Cromwell helped to create, and which created him.

'Undoubtedly this is the most intelligent summation we
have on Cromwell, and it is written with the grace
and power we have come to expect from Dr Hill' –
J.P. Kenyon in the *Observer*

'A humane and imaginative book by a historian writing
at the peak of his powers, coping from long experience
with the difficulties of a hectic age' – Ivan Roots in the
Daily Telegraph

'God's Englishman is a very fine book' – J.H. Plumb in the
Guardian

The Law of Freedom and Other Writings

Gerrard Winstanley

EDITED BY CHRISTOPHER HILL

Leader of the Diggers, or True Levellers, whose colony
was forced to disband in 1651, Gerrard Winstanley
stands out from a century remarkable for its developments
in political thought as one of the most fecund and original
of political writers. An acute and penetrating social
critic with a passionate sense of justice, he worked out
a collectivist theory which strikingly anticipates nineteenth
and twentieth-century socialism. Although other writers
had proposed the reconstruction of the whole social order
on rational principles, Winstanley was the first to put
forward such a programme in the vernacular and to call
upon the oppressed to translate it into action. Christopher
Hill's selection of his many published pamphlets demonstrates
the coherence and social relevance of Winstanley's
philosophy while it reveals his mastery of colloquial
prose and superb use of imagery.

A History of Soviet Russia

E. H. Carr

This monumental work has emerged as a masterly survey of
the political, social and economic history of the early
days of Soviet Russia: an outstanding and lucidly written
analysis, richer in detail and wider in scope than even
Carr first envisaged. It is a consummate work of scholarship
which no student of Russia can afford to be without
and which the general reader will be delighted to own
and enjoy.

So far published in Penguins are:

THE BOLSHEVIK REVOLUTION 1917–23

Volume 1

Volume 2: The Economic Order
Volume 3: Soviet Russia and the World

THE INTERREGNUM 1923–24

SOCIALISM IN ONE COUNTRY 1924–26

in three volumes

FOUNDATIONS OF A PLANNED ECONOMY 1926–29

Volume 1 (with R. W. Davis)
Volume 2

'The style is luminous, the architecture of the entire work
is beautifully proportioned; the exposition is always
interesting ... And the whole work is the most important
contribution made to its subject ... in any language' – *Sunday Times*

also by E. H. Carr

What is History?